Things We Leave Behind

Josephine Balmer studied Classics and Ancient History at University College, London and has a PhD in Literature and Creative Writing from the University of East Anglia. As well as five poetry collections, she has also published translations of Sappho (revised 2018), an anthology of classical women poets (1996) and Catullus (2004), alongside a study of creative translation, *Piecing Together the Fragments* (2013). She has acted as Chair of the Society of Authors Translators Association and a judge for the Stephen Spender Prize, as well as Reviews Editor for the journal *Modern Poetry in Translation*.

Paschalis Nikolaou is Associate Professor in Literary Translation at the Ionian University, Greece, and author of *The Return of Pytheas: Scenes from British and Greek Poetry in Dialogue* (2017) and *Creative Classical Translation* (2023).

Things We Leave Behind
—Selected Poems—

Josephine Balmer

Edited and introduced by
Paschalis Nikolaou

Shearsman Books

First published in the United Kingdom in 2025 by
Shearsman Books Ltd
PO Box 4239   Swindon   SN3 9FN

Shearsman Books Ltd Registered Office
30–31 St. James Place, Mangotsfield, Bristol BS16 9JB
(this address not for correspondence)

EU AUTHORISED REPRESENTATIVE:
Lightning Source France, 1 Av. Johannes Gutenberg, 78310 Maurepas, France
Email: compliance@lightningsource.fr

ISBN 978-1-83738-003-9

ACKNOWLEDGEMENTS

Poems from *Chasing Catullus: Poems, Translations and Transgressions*
are reproduced by kind permission of Bloodaxe Books.

Poems from *The Word for Sorrow*
are reproduced by kind permission of Salt Publishing.

Poems from *Letting Go: thirty mourning sonnets and two poems*
are reproduced by kind permission of Agenda Editions.

The Paths of Survival and *Ghost Passage* were published by Shearsman Books.

'Geometric' was first published in *Arion,* 'Odysseus and Laertes' and 'Catalogues,
Various' in *New Statesman*, 'Reading the Signals' in *Agenda* and 'Burying the
Bones' in *Shearsman* magazine. 'Preparing to Meet the Dead' and 'Worth' were
first published in a signature pamphlet, *Unquiet Churches*, by Seamarks Press.

Sincere thanks are due to Neil Astley, Suzanne Fairless-Aitken, Chris Hamilton-
Emery, Patricia McCarthy, Kelvin Corcoran and Tony Frazer.

And, finally, many thanks to Emily Young for permission to reproduce her
sculpture on the cover.

Contents

The Paths of Survival (2017)

Letting Go: thirty mourning sonnets and two poems (2017)

Ghost Passage (2022)

Archaeology of Home (new poems)

Introduction

'Ancient literature – by which I mean classical Greek and Latin literature – must always be re-created,' the scholar and translator D.S. Carne-Ross has commented, 'the sentence, often the word, has to be dissolved, atomized, and its elements then reconstituted in a new form'.[1] Josephine Balmer's poetry has long been concerned with this reconstitution of the written word. Ever since 2004's *Chasing Catullus*, which articulates contemporary grief through ancient texts and voices, Balmer has engaged in a ceaseless dialogue with the past, laying era on era, text on text. 'Poetry and History meet,' W.S. Milne has written of her work, 'not competing for once, but brilliantly fused and celebrated'.[2]

Balmer's early practice as a translator of classical poetry is central here. In 1984, shortly after completing a BA in Classics at University College, London, the then 25-year-old produced *Sappho: Poems and Fragments*, initially published by Brilliance Books but later reissued in revised editions for Bloodaxe (1992 & 2018). In 1996, *Classical Women Poets* assembled neglected female poetic voices, from archaic Greece to the late Roman empire. Both volumes engaged with the fragmentation of their source texts, an issue which would later become crucial in Balmer's own poetry. Both also excavate forgotten and overlooked voices which, again, would play its part in her later collections. In 2004 she turned to the more complete, if often scatological and occasionally sexually violent, verse of the Roman male poet, Catullus, an act of transgendered ventriloquism which would reappear throughout her poetic work. In her introduction to *Catullus: Poems of Love and Hate*, she notes how the Roman poet adopted, and adapted, tone, voice and metres from earlier Greek poets, particularly Sappho whose 'meltingly erotic imagery' he translated – and transformed.[3] Even in the classical era, it seems, original poems could themselves already be palimpsests.

On the same day that *Catullus: Poems of Love and Hate* appeared, Balmer also published her own first collection *Chasing Catullus* – that slimmer volume of 'poems, translations and transgressions' – whose genius lies in the exploitation of a range of interpretive positions, con-solidating Balmer's expressive intent. Examples range from partial translations interleaved across the poems 'Niobe' (p.31) or 'Letchworth Crematorium' (p.41) and pieces that pile source on source, such as 'Cancel the Invite II' (p.32) which takes inspiration from T.S. Eliot's 'Little

Gidding' in versioning a passage of Plato's *Republic*, to contemplations of painting in dialogue with ancient myth ('After Titian's *Bacchus and Ariadne*', p.27). Such creative con-versing chronicles a fatal illness and its impact on a family: the three sections of *Chasing Catullus* – 'Before', 'During' and 'After' – follow the story of Balmer's niece, dying from liver cancer. Now, translating, and versioning, classical texts 'became the vocabulary through which I could begin to say the unsayable. To approach events and emotions that might otherwise have been too distressing to articulate'.[4] In this sense, the proximity of poems directly addressing her niece's diagnosis, for example '*De Raptu Proserpinae*' (p.30), which reworks a passage from Claudian describing Persephone's abduction by Pluto, helps to avoid some of the usual trappings of confessional poetry. Although raw emotion is still often present. We read 'In Coventry' (p.35), set in the city's cathedral: 'Still I've not come for absolution, / but to curse the hand that could make / her cells divide, multiply / and stop ours from reproducing…'. Similarly, 'Demeter in Winter' (p.34) begins: 'And my grief is hardening, blade by blade / with the grass […]'.

While individual poems like 'Philomela' (p.29) suggest the potency of contemporary verse accessing classical sources – we witness this, too, in work by Simon Armitage or A.E. Stallings – it is the architectural ambition, the dialogic scope of *Chasing Catullus* that points to Balmer's unique poetic voice. Her language, 'fluid and direct, resolutely set on establishing contact with the reader, counterbalances the sophistication of her overall design', as I wrote in an early review.[5] This continued stance also owes a debt to T.S. Eliot, an avowed influence (especially the Eliot of *Four Quartets*), yet produces different emphases – as can be seen in the course of this timely *Selected Poems*, which samples all of Balmer's published collections, as well as eight new poems from a forthcoming volume, *Archaeology of Home*.

The consequential weaving of originals and translation progresses in a sophomore volume, *The Word for Sorrow*, which intertwines versions of the Roman poet Ovid with the story of the old, second-hand dictionary being used to translate them. Balmer was drawn originally to Ovid's epistolary verse in *Tristia* and *Epistulae ex Ponto*, written following his exile from Rome to the Black Sea in CE 8 ('a rare moment when the mask of classical literary artifice slips away to reveal the raw pain of the man beneath' as her preface puts it[6]). Working on some versions during an electrical storm, with the internet down, Balmer turned to an old second-hand dictionary. An inscription on its flyleaf (and a subsequent Google search) identifies a British soldier in the Gallipoli campaign as the dictionary's original owner. So now Balmer's poetic mind starts to trace how '[a]ccounts detailing the sickness, deprivations and dangers of the Gallipoli campaign in which 50,000 Allied troops and 85,000 Turkish soldiers died, seemed reminiscent of Ovid's powerful laments about his own exile'.[7]

The initial engagement with translating Ovid's exile verse develops into another structure of successive time-frames (in three parts: 'The Journey Out', 'Landed', 'The Way Home') in which various edits of Ovid's exile meditations, and new poems – often 'found' through documents from Gallipoli – spark off each other. 'Dancing in the Dark' (p.47) directly quotes *Epistulae ex Ponto* 4.2.32-4; 'Between the Lines' (p.50) is based on a soldier's letter recounting conditions of living – and dying – in the trenches. In the opening of 'Landed' (p.49) there is no hiding from the absurdity and carnage: 'For a prize of dirt, a few yards of scrub, / they fought like gods as soil soaked red, / shallows curdled, stagnant with corpse-shoals.' Ovid's mood and register changes often but this is also true of the soldiers' letters home. In a review for *Poetry London*, Kate Bingham calls this 'a kind of docupoem, a collage of voices in which authenticity is as important as art'.[8] Again, translation is important here: in 'Seeking Quarter' (p.57), a version of lines from *Tristia* 4.4 precedes a stanza where Balmer compares the travails of Ovid with those of the British soldier. Such compounds reveal how the writer's work evolves throughout *The Word for Sorrow*. As Balmer told Lorna Hardwick:

> Ovid's *Tristia* started to bleed into my original text and that happened more and more as the work went on. I found myself merging the two. It was as if the boundaries broke down as I was in the act of writing the collection because it does have a narrative drive and I did tend to write it in the order in which it appeared. So the more I engaged with Ovid, the more he started appearing in my original poems.[9]

A collapsing of time ensues: in 'Naso All at Sea' (p.46; Ovid calls himself 'Naso' in his poems), for instance, Ovid's predicament as he approaches Tomis, his place of exile, parallels the soldier's letters and reminiscences of 'Welcome Note' (p.56). Earlier in the collection, the two halves of 'Malvern Road Station, Cheltenham' (p.48), dated April 1915 and February 2005, compare the soldiers' grim experiences with Balmer's own feelings of resignation as she visits their departure point for the war, now long-demolished. These poems are miniatures of the entire book.

Such paralleling ultimately conveys – Balmer hopes – 'wider, universal tragedies. Most important of all, though, are the links forged between ancient and modern, past and present, the invisible lines that connect us to often surprising points in history, finding common ground in unexpected places, celebrating the common humanity that binds us, whether we live at the beginning of the first, the twentieth or the twenty-first century CE'.[10] The last few poems in *The Word for Sorrow*, 'The Penny Pot' as well as the collection's title poem (pp.60 and 61-63), suggest that family history, too, motivates Balmer's linking of Tomis and Gallipoli.

As in *Chasing Catullus*'s titular poem (p.28), *The Word for Sorrow*'s 'Dictionary Definitions' (p.54) explores contours of translation as the meaning and context of ancient words leads to solemn insights: 'This shroud of Latin: **amissus. mortuus.** / The dragging, leaden cloak of language: / *missing in action, presumed dead.*' The Ovid poems in *The Word for Sorrow*, Balmer tells us, should resemble 'pages from a translator's notebook, detailed sketches before the finished original'.[11] Here, for instance, Balmer first comes to explore 'an interaction between translation and translator-as-narrator'.[12] Questions of gender also persist; in the Introduction to *Catullus: Poems of Love and Hate*, Balmer reveals that she resisted temptation, as a twenty-first century woman, to subvert Catullus' male Roman sensibilities as he himself had done with Sappho's 'essentially female poetics in his cross-gendered versions'.[13] As she notes: 'perhaps, as a woman, I could not take his belligerent posturing too seriously.' When the frame and intent become more literary in Balmer's own collections, however, gender is frequently transgressed or transcended as *The Word for Sorrow* so vividly illustrates in the voices of both 'Geoffrey' and 'Naso' alongside her own. But this process begins as early as 'Fresh Meat' from *Chasing Catullus* (described as 'a perversion of *Iliad* 22', p.37-38), where the poem is ventriloquised through the male voice of the Trojan hero Hector. Later, in 'Let Go', the poet's late mother assumes the form of Aeneas's dead wife Creusa in a passage of Virgil's *Aeneid* (p.107). In an interview with Fiona Cox, Balmer details how this then 'cast me, in turn, as Aeneas'.[14]

Dialogues with poetry also interest Balmer in her scholarly and critical writing. *Piecing Together the Fragments: Translating Classical Verse, Creating Contemporary Poetry*, her study for the Oxford Classical Presences series, casts translation as an accelerant to the poetic process. Balmer's many reviews for newspapers and literary journals over the years reveal her own poetic influences (as do those commissioned between 2004 and 2009 as reviews editor of *Modern Poetry in Translation*). In a 2016 piece for *New Statesman*, she traces Seamus Heaney's engagement with *Aeneid* Book VI through poems from 1991's *Seeing Things* and 2010's *Human Chain*, to his posthumously published rendering of Virgil's epic.[15] Reviewing Anne Carson's radical version of Sophocles, *Antigonick*, for *The Times* in 2012, Balmer notes that 'Carson's version represents both a reading and a writing; it enacts not only the text itself but its reception, its resonances'.[16] This can also be said of Balmer's own poems. She has often written about Michael Longley's recastings of classical literature which can be counted among her influences – and, in turn, Longley admitted privately that *Classical Women Poets* inspired parts of his collection, *Snow Water* (2004). Missing pieces also spur the poetry; in an essay about newly-found papyrus fragments, and how they led her to revise *Sappho: Poems and Fragments*, Balmer anticipates that the next few years might well see

> more fragments coming to light which will negate the transla-
> tions here, both new and old. But this is not only to be expected
> but welcomed. Each new version marks a new staging point in
> an ancient text's long, long history. Each one represents Pound's
> 'blood brought to ghosts', each performs an act of poetic necro-
> mancy, conjuring up fresh, breathing poems.[17]

Such awareness informs many of her lines – the ground plan even, in some collections. In 2017's *The Paths of Survival*, an almost completely lost play by Aeschylus, *Myrmidons*, is imagined into poetry, moving backwards in time from a scrap of papyrus in a present-day library through the dramatic monologues of the various actors involved in its preservation or erasures, its later editing and transmissions. Named in brief sections, almost all of them comprising two poems (the present book draws one from each section), those 'Editors', 'Anthologists', 'Translators', 'Annotators' exist as stages in our collective relationship with a phantasmic text. We glimpse *Myrmidons* mostly in relay, and through the writing of others: from accounts of the Oxyrhynchus papyrus scraps containing incomplete lines in 'The Student's Find', (p.70-71), to Lucian of Samosata brooding on his legacy while comparing himself to Homer and Aeschylus ('*Erotic Tales*', p.78), and an Oxford classical scholar reflecting on his 'Redaction' (p.72) of a line from *Myrmidons*. These verse-episodes from (literary) history featuring custodians and re-makers of the tragedy, suggest an unbroken community. Threading them kaleidoscopically together, *The*

Paths of Survival names a desire we share for the work of salvage, itself a reason behind much of Balmer's poetry. Nowhere is this clearer than in the middle stanza of 'The Librarians' Power' (p.68-69), accounting for their actions in war-ravaged Baghdad, 2003:

> We were asked why we struggled
> to save books while all around us
> so many of our citizens were lost.
> We could only say that, if not flesh,
> here were dividing cells, bare blocks
> of collective memory. Conscience.

Balmer's monologues are precisely phrased, presenting different lengths, formations and influences (for instance, Heaney's 'sonnet and a half' in the twenty-one lines of 'The Ferryman's Roll', p.82).[18] The language remains colloquial and direct, despite the reverse chronology, arriving finally at the Greek dramatist revising *Myrmidons* on his deathbed in Gela, Sicily, in 456 BCE. In 'Aeschylus' Revision' (p.84-89), he thinks back on his experience of the battle of Marathon, and his own passion for his fellow soldier, Cynaegirus, which, in Balmer's version, inspires his version of the love story of the Homeric heroes Achilles and Patroclus in his play. In the process, he shares with us anxieties about his writing ('And Greek is too vague, the language / of the colour blind […]' p.84). Then, as an epilogue to the collection, the few surviving pieces of *Myrmidons'* text come to meet us in English translation, with Balmer's annotations on facing pages. A séance of an original before the centuries of its resonances, and a talismanic translation augmented and completed by the heap of imagined voices that precede it.

These monologues are fueled by scholarship; a fertile associating of the creative and the critical enables much of Balmer's freer and hybrid work, helping her to arrive at ideas about form or framing. To take one example, 'Margin' (p.80-81), containing an annotator's musings on comic parodies of Aeschylus, is itself laid out on the margin of the page. This goes beyond a poignant use of poetic form as mimesis; Vassilis Lambropoulos has argued that by drawing on

> a variety of poetic forms, techniques, meters, and sources, Balmer achieves something rare, a classicizing theory-in-verse of classical (and literary in general) reception – a theory of classical

reception in poetic form and through practices of classical reception. This is neither mere reception nor mere theory but a poetic theorization of what goes under 'classical reception' in both scholarship and translation.[19]

Conversely, Balmer's journals and academic volume contributions often adopt a practitioner's perspective. 'The Library versus The Lyre', her essay for a special issue of *Synthesis* edited by myself, concludes: '…without scholarship *Myrmidons* would be lost. And without poetry it would never have been written.'[20]

The appearance of *Letting Go* a mere month after *The Paths of Survival*, recalls the simultaneous publication of the Catullus translations and *Chasing Catullus*. An elegy for Balmer's mother, these thirty sonnets amalgamate versioned and quoted text by a sizable cast of classical authors: 'Suppliants' (p.95) is announced as 'ghosting Aeschylus' and his *Suppliant Women*, recognising a language of lament across time; ancient weather conditions reflect stages of mourning through glimpses from the *Iliad* or Livy's *The History of Rome* in 'Snow' (p.97), 'Ice' (p.99), and 'Thaw' (p.101). 'Fairfield Church' (p.102) collapses time and geography through lines from Pausanias on the entrance to the Underworld ('Below, the marsh channels coiled like the Styx'; 'This time all the birds of Kent and Sussex / have fallen silent as if Avernus, / the poisoned gate to Hell, lay beneath us'). Identifications of this kind contrast with the larger-scale chronicle of a literary absence in *The Paths of Survival* – and its more communal piecing of the picture – turning the memory of her lost parent into an event outside time: 'Seat' (p.106), set on the coastal footpath between Marazion and Perranuthnoe, loved by mother and daughter, opens with lines by Odysseus in the court of Alcinous, recalling how much he misses Ithaca. In 'By-pass' (p.103), a passage from *Plato's Symposium* on Orpheus and Eurydice also conveys the poet's own sorrow in present-day Cornwall: 'So the gods sent punishment we deserved; / this quagmire grief that serves as its own curse. / The pain you cannot write through or by-pass. / That feels like too little love. Or too much.'

'Things We Leave Behind' (p.93) – in which a favourite family table is given to charity and accidentally seen again – is modelled after C.P. Cavafy, the Greek poet born in Alexandria and the only modern literary voice present in *Letting Go*. The absent lover who haunts the verses of Cavafy's 'The Afternoon Sun' from 1919 is replaced with memories of the poet's dead mother, as well as typical British town scenes and locales (we read of 'dust-blanched builders' in the café, 'slumped over strong tea, the full English, / as dark and heady as funeral incense'). Other lines are extracted from the Greek poem ('*They must always have been around somewhere, those worn-out old things…*'), but even when not quoted, Cavafy provides a register – especially in several sonnets, where classical references recede in favour of everyday items invoking the lost loved one ('Ring', p.96, 'Glove', p.98, 'Watch' p.100). Indeed, Cavafy is present from the very first pages of *Chasing Catullus*. Here '*78 Nights*' (p.25) transplants his 1907 poem 'One Night' in to the late 1970s London of Balmer's student days:

> From the window all you could see was the brick walk
> by railway arch. But throughout that distilled summer,
> voices drifted up, wind-sent from the street below –
> workmen, hacks, GLC clerks in C&A suits,
> flushed on gassy beer and pressure-pump wine, the short
> measure triumphs of pool and darts, trivial pursuits.

Balmer has spoken about the Alexandrian poet's childhood years spent in Liverpool (where her father was born), and how crucial a similar treatment of 'small situations' from ancient history has been in her work.[21] The mode is also unmistakable when she crafts *The Paths of Survival*, particularly in 'The Christians' Cheek' (p.77) or 'Aeschylus' Desk' (p.83). A Cavafian tenor continues in Balmer's next collection, assisting her to conjure the Roman substrata of a modern metropolis in poems such as 'The First European' (p.112) or 'Thief' (p.116-117). *Ghost Passage*'s first two sections ('In Wood', 'Through Clay') are populated by thoroughly imagined human voices assigned the scant words scrawled across inscribed material artefacts: wooden writing tablets, excavated during the building of the new Bloomberg Headquarters in the City of London, as well as marble slabs, pots, tiles, seals, even pewter amulets, discovered elsewhere in the city.

A third section, 'On Stone (Oxney Sonnets)', returns to variations of a familiar form, and afterimages of cultures in contention with each other. It also returns the poet to the concerns of previous collections: wartime churchyard graves are found in 'Jazz' (p.126) and 'A Few Feet' (p.127); 'Visitors' Book' (p.128) revolves around an inscription by Balmer's mother in Snargate church. It ends: '…Less than six weeks left with her / before our dates, our lines, will be taken by / be these others, thickened with different scripts: / pilgrims, walkers, ancestor worshipers.'

Churches and surrounding spaces have been contemplated before, as 'In Coventry' and 'Fairfield Church' attest. But there is a cumulative effect here, running through to the forthcoming *Archaeology of Home*. Throughout *Ghost Passage*, arresting imagery suggests how similar thoughts occur across time in the same geographical space:

We have seen our city shrink to sand
so we scratch wood to soothe the ache –
diminished words we leave behind
to score these shuddering, ghosted streets
back into form and place: *London writer.*
    ('Writer [?] London', p.111)

In large part, the book acts on this statement, a printed extension of that excavation site. Balmer foregrounds materials used to record interactions across social layers (as well as the writing tablets, an inscribed stylus from 75 CE found in Walbrook in 'Keepsake', (p.118) or a marble slab in 'Seafarer' (p.121). The task the poet sets herself is to explore how these minds, their worries and wishes inside a speculative Roman London, may be felt in our present, and instruct us. It is poetry that answers whether an 'archaeological horizon' – the layer of soil covering sites of London – indicates, as we read in the note for 'Dark Earth' (p.122), 'abandonment or continuous occupation':

Decay crept outwards from centre to edge
but we held firm, jeering at those who fled.
Markets crashed so we buried our money.
Sickness shadowed us on the streets. We stayed
at home. In time we knew nothing of towns
beyond our own. Squares, gardens, all spare land
we turned to crops. Fights were stopped, games not played.
In the arena baiting bears ran free.

These fictional ancient lives are treated with the same compassion and care shown towards the real people mentioned in, or writing the documents from, the Gallipoli campaign in *The Word for Sorrow* and its 'found poems'. Interviewed after *Ghost Passage*'s publication, Balmer lists the diversity of the classical world and Roman London as a point she wanted to transmit to readers: the book 'has Greek, Syrian, African and Celtic citizens as well as Romano-British, all found in the sources'[22]

('Will', p.115, especially reflects this). The poet shows us how mundane daily obligations, and their associated artifacts, are as worthy of our attention as the ancient dramas and epics. *Ghost Passage* indeed includes comment on how memory and empathy are enabled by the technologies of writing. Writing is also how change is affirmed, as we read in 'New Roman' (p.114), which alludes to the Boudica revolt:

> We do not want this world, the old language:
> *destruction, put to fire, revolt, flight, death.*
> Our task is to etch a new alphabet:
> new letters, new tools to rebuild our homes,
> gardens for us children, games to play. Schools.
> We'll smooth the jagged edge of dialect
> and salve its gaping wounds in majuscule.

The new poems included here from a work-in-progress, *Archaeology of Home*, perfectly sum up this poet's preoccupations: dedicated to Balmer's late father (present also in several sonnets from *Letting Go*), the distances between personal and collective loss collapse more often, and more radically, here. A first sequence takes us through notions of absence and (re)discovery of persons and cultures in the classical world (as, for example, in 'Writing Cure', p.131). This attends to several incidents between fathers and children ('Odysseus and Laertes', p.132, is just one example), in particular the loss of memory and onset of dementia in an elderly parent, both ancient and modern. Just as in *Ghost Passage*, poems like 'Geometric' (p.133) arrive at illuminations through excavated finds: 'Here, in clay, all rules are now broken; the terrible / knowledge of what we no longer know. The angled path / to our shrinking past. *The whole is greater than the part.*' Then, in a titular sequence of twelve poems, reminiscent of *Letting Go* (of which two are included here), Balmer rummages through her parents' belongings as she clears her father's house, reflecting a thought the poet shared in an interview with Leslie Tate:

> […] historians and archaeologists have more in common with poets than might at first appear. Both seek to uncover lost fragments of human existence, the detritus we leave behind, whether physical or emotional. Both forge connections between past and present, inevitably and inescapably reading that past in terms of our present. And where archaeology excavates beautiful, lost

objects, long-buried in the accumulating silt of history, poetry excavates language, particularly image and metaphor, from the dusty inspiration of time and place. Both meticulously brush away the dirt to restore the colour and vibrancy to long-forgotten or discarded artefacts. Above all, both seek to reconstruct the tattered fragments. To rebuild the fallen cities. To give breath to the silent voices.[23]

The idea is applied to the microcosm of family relationships with the same empathy as it is to the macrocosm of human civilization. In the wake of her father's passing, Balmer observes their 'Daffodil Vase' (p.134) in a similar manner to the artefacts encountered in museums or archaeological sites: 'As if a faded Roman fresco, only the stalks are left.' There is admirable technical control across the 'restorations' that make up *Archaeology of Home*, and the poems included here are more terse than before, epigrammatic, urgent. In 'Catalogues, Various' (p.135), the leaflets still arriving by post at the family house are remindful of her father's absence. On his last day (as seen again by the poet in a dream): 'He slings me a brochure for The Far, Far North / slippery as verglas. *See*, he says. *I've already left.*'

A second sequence expands on the concerns that guided, in part, *The Word for Sorrow*. But now 'The Blood Road' explores ancient conflicts that can still resonate with us. This sequence was first published in *Long Poem Magazine*, where Balmer described how its underlying classical sources allowed her 'to approach the almost inexpressible horror of present brutalities, underscoring how the relentless churn of violence rattles down through the centuries'.[24] 'Reading the Signals' (p.136) and 'Burying the Bones' (p.137), the sequence's first and last poems (both included here), draw on, respectively, a 513 BCE clash between the Persians and the Scythians in the Sea of Azov, and a Roman general in Teutoburg, visiting the site of a disastrous defeat of imperial legionaries by Germanic tribes in 15 CE, marking how ancient massacres bleed into current atrocities.

Following the warfare that permeates this middle sequence, in 'Unquiet Churches' Balmer returns to the concerns of her Oxney sonnets, contemplating residual consciousness inside and around sacred structures that themselves often grow over the centuries. In 'Preparing to Meet the Dead' (p.138), the poet reflects on Boscawen-ûn, an ancient stone circle in West Penwith, observing how a central shaft leans 'towards a grave slumped in its own passage; / a signpost for the lost – to Tartarus – / pointing out the way with its carved bare feet'. In 'Worth' (p. 139), one of the oldest churches in England leads to a striking description of the passage of time that starts with a quote from the Anglo-Saxon of 'The Wanderer':

> *Wyrd changes the changing world.* Time folds. Then.
> Now. Every year for the last thousand
> the sun has brushed the glass to spot the stones
> just here: viridian, cobalt, crimson…
> Each has their worth. But light still wanes. Moves on.

While Balmer has drawn on sources beyond the classical world before, in the wake of *Ghost Passage*'s Roman London, *Archaeology of Home* involves further sediments of British history, its languages and literatures.

The dozen or more poems drawn from each of the five collections that Balmer has published – with the kind permission of Salt Publishing, Bloodaxe Books and Agenda Editions – show her gift for enlivening ancient voices, as well as an imaginative recasting of classical sources so that they seep into the present; a past that teaches, and consoles. This poetry is at its most indispensable as we commune with emotions and experiences often concealed rather than unveiled by translation. As Balmer's title poem in *Chasing Catullus* (p.28) jokingly explains: 'It's the rule of attraction, the corruption of texts, / the way his corpus tastes of skin and sweat.' *Things We Leave Behind* further intimates the much considered design of Balmer's collections whose quality often lies in their ordering and accumulation of voices and source texts. Their original accompanying notes and comments are also included in full at the end of this *Selected Poems*, with minor emendations. Notes form an aspect of Balmer's literary enterprise and often disclose a fascinating process, and inspirations, even as most of this verse can be enjoyed without reaching for them.

The pages that follow are replete with recognitions of cultural crisis points and survivals, animating the poetry. Whole sequences revolve on the fragility and transience of our bodies, the disseminations of human thought, the losses and finds of all our endeavours, personal and collective. Balmer has mined, more consistently than most, the grey zones between versifying and translating, and the ways in which the self connects with the main instrument of its expression. Her collections *Ghost Passage* and

The Paths of Survival especially, but many individual poems too, narrate ecologies of human consciousness across history's vast plains, BCE to the dawn of a new millennium. Her achievement lies in the ways in which this verse affirms, time and again, as 'The Librarians' Power' celebrates: 'Our own enduring, unshakable belief / that in each newly-deciphered letter / A poem waited to be recovered.'

Notes

[1] D.S. Carne-Ross, 'Translation and Transposition', in *The Craft and Context of Translation: A Symposium*, eds. William Arrowsmith and Roger Shattuck (Austin: University of Texas Press, for Humanities Research Center, 1961), p.4.

[2] W.S. Milne, 'Digging Deep: Josephine Balmer, *The Paths of Survival*', *Agenda* 51 (January 2018; online reviews supplement: 'Essays/Reviews in tandem with the special T.S. Eliot issue, Vol. 51, No 3-4'). Available at: https://agendapoetry.co.uk/documents/TSEliotOnlineEssays.pdf

[3] Josphine Balmer, 'Introduction', *Catullus: Poems of Love and Hate* (Tarset: Bloodaxe Books, 2004), p.18.

[4] Josephine Balmer and Leslie Tate, 'History, and the Power of Poetry to Give Breath to the Silent Voices: Part One' (3 April 2023). Available at: https://leslietate.com/2023/04/03/17179/

[5] Paschalis Nikolaou, 'Translating Ancient Passions', *The London Magazine* (April/ May 2005), p.106.

[6] Josephine Balmer, 'Preface', *The Word for Sorrow* (Cambridge: Salt Publishing, 2009), p.xiii.

[7] 'Preface', *ibid.*

[8] Kate Bingham, 'Reports of Recovery', *Poetry London* 65 (2009), p.30.

[9] 'Josephine Balmer and Lorna Hardwick, 'Josephine Balmer, Poet and Translator, in Interview with Lorna Hardwick' (Oxford, 17th May 2010)', *Practitioners' Voices in Classical Reception* 2 (September 2010). Available at: https://university.open.ac.uk/arts/research/pvcrs/2010/balmer

[10] 'Preface', p. xvii.

[11] 'Preface', p. xvi.

[12] Josephine Balmer, *Piecing Together the Fragments: Translating Classical Verse, Creating Contemporary Poetry* (Oxford: Oxford University Press, 2013), p.201.

[13] 'Introduction', *Catullus: Poems of Love and Hate*, p.24.

[14] Josephine Balmer, Fiona Cox and Elena Theodorakopoulos, 'Remaking ancient Greek and Roman myths in the twenty-first century: Jo Balmer', *Practitioners' Voices in Classical Reception* 8 (2017). Available at: https://university.open. ac.uk/arts/research/pvcrs/2017/balmer.

[15] Josephine Balmer, 'Seamus Heaney's translation of *Aeneid* Book VI: a fitting end to a life's work', *New Statesman* (6 April 2016), p.43.

[16] 'Josephine Balmer, 'Antigonick: Anne Carson', *The Times* (2 June 2012). Available at: https://archive.ph/nvPAj

[17] Josephine Balmer, 'The New Fragments: Texts, Translations and Retranslations', *Sappho: Poems and Fragments* (Tarset: Bloodaxe Books, 2018), p.45.

[18] Josephine Balmer, 'The Library versus the Lyre: *The Paths of Survival* and the Poetry of Textual History', *Synthesis* 12 (2020; 'Anglophone Presences of Classical Literature' ed. Paschalis Nikolaou), p.88.

[19] Vassilis Lambropoulos, 'Theory in Verse', *Piano Poetry Pantelis Politics* (11 February 2018). Available at: https://poetrypiano.wordpress.com/2018/02/11/ theory-in-verse/

[20] 'The Library versus the Lyre: *The Paths of Survival* and the Poetry of Textual History', p.93.

[21] See Balmer and Hardwick, p. 7.

[22] Josephine Balmer and Leslie Tate, 'History, and the Power of Poetry to Give Breath to the Silent Voices: Part Two' (10 April 2023). Available at: https:// leslietate.com/2023/04/10/joephine-balmer-and-the-power-of-poetry-to-give-breath-to-the-silent-voices-part-two/

[23] See Balmer and Tate, 'History, and the Power of Poetry to Give Breath to the Silent Voices: Part One'.

[24] Josephine Balmer, 'The Blood Road', *Long Poem Magazine* 29 (Spring 2023), p.13.

Chasing Catullus:
Poems, Translations and Transgressions

(2004)

'78 Nights
(*after Cavafy*)

The room was dingy, always damp and dark – but cheap,
hard to find, down the alley by the Courage pub.
From the window all you could see was the brick walk
by railway arch. But throughout that distilled summer,
voices drifted up, wind-sent from the street below –
workmen, hacks, GLC clerks in C&A suits,
flushed on gassy beer and pressure-pump wine, the short
measure triumphs of pool and darts, trivial pursuits.

And there, on that sweated, sagging, second-hand bed,
we shared one body, one soul, till your lips became
my own, rose – no, the deep brown-red of vintage wine,
the stain that lingers long after the glass is drained,
so even now – years later – as I write alone
in my High Weald house, damp and dark and deep brown-red,
I'm drunk again on that same taste, same touch, same smell,
reeling once more at the red, red lies they could tell.

Feminine Ending: to Sulpicia

Midnight in Rome, summer, the year one,
and you're going home, the party's fading fast:
you've defiled aediles, procured a procurator,
got a handful of jokes past the stern new censor
(if not amused when you declined his parts).
Even the emperor, not noted for humour,
put your best up with – let's think – Tibullus:
all right, the man's a bore, a pain, a total ass,
but there could be worse ways to share a *floruit*:
a whole new world now, new empires to crush,
you see, you're famous, a star, fêted genius.

But empires fold, dates blur, years move on,
and you're marginalised, anthologised – just;
you've evaded Vandals, survived the Huns,
got a handful of poems past the monks and nuns,
if they still removed each *Sulpicia est*;
even academia, not noted for humour,
put your best down to – let's think – Tibullus:
 all right, you know the score, the same old *caveat*:
your work can't exist, or, if it does, it's trash;
just the way of the world, survival of the fittest;
you see, your name ends in 'a' and they want 'us'.

After Titian's *Bacchus and Ariadne*

(…their hand guides the brush with more confidence.
The same for the translator…)

Already she's pointing to the stars.

She's had enough of earth-bound schemes,
of mapping out the boundless maze,
disentangling all their secret themes,
to be called faithless, traitor, tart.
So when the god leaps out into the void,
as if strength and youth can fill the gap –
could compensate for theft or lust –
she'll turn and smile and take the cup.

Beyond, the faithful, fired by frenzy,
the passion that can alter words and minds;
they wave their cymbals, each sacred point,
scatter sacrificial flesh, engrossed, spell-bound.
And dreaming deep in dust-bowl caskets,
the sense most search their lives in vain to find…

What Titian read in his Catullus
and Auerbach scraped in turn from Titian,
what Ariadne somehow always knew:
that equivalence will cancel loss,
difference fade in abstract vision;
that all form, all shape, can be reduced
to these four truths:
                              yellow
          red   green

          and blue.

Chasing Catullus

It's the rule of attraction, the corruption of texts,
the way his corpus tastes of skin and sweat,
that taint of decay, scent of cheated death.

But then, I've always liked them old –
parsed hearts, lost minds, redundant souls;
just enough to get me fleshing ghosts,
giving them tongue, jumping their bones.

Yet sleep with the dead and you'll wake
with the worms – stripped down, compressed,
a little accusative, slightly stressed – to find
the code you crack, the clause that breaks,
is no longer subordinate, it's now your own.

Philomela

One way or another, I'd have done it myself.
Let grief, guilt or prick-sharp shame
wear down my tongue to a bloody stump;
slit my own throat, sliced off my lips,
in case my traitor speech should shape that place again.

So now I weave my words with crimson thread,
pick out my stunted songs in sacking cords –
the music of the deaf, the music of the dead.
And my soul frays at the plan I start to trace;
homes blocked in by sex and strife and sword,
the husband dropped, wife I'll never make.

And my heart knots at the thought of kids:
they seem too soft, too sweet, too pure to stitch.

De Raptu Proserpinae
(2/8: 6.47AM)

Now she came to the hills wound round and round
in grass. At first light she picked her flowers:
the earth shivered with dew, violets slaked
their new-born thirst. But as the Sun advanced
on its high noon sky, night fell like a thief
and our land trembled to the touch, trampled,
dust-blown, under four sets of cloven hooves.
Their horseman we didn't know – harbinger,
camp-follower, or even Death Himself –
but now our soft meadows bruised, rivers stopped
mid-flow, fields rusted like forgotten ploughs.
To breathe was suicide: trees drained of green,
roses shed their petals, lilies shrivelled
before our eyes. And then He turned away,
swinging round the reins like the gates of Hell
grating to a close. Night scuttled after
as the light seeped back into our black world
        – everywhere was light
        sun and sky and light –
and your small daughter nowhere to be seen.

Niobe

(2/8: 7.22AM)

(*after Sophocles*)

Like a cloud-burst on a Penwith day
that had to come yet still startles, shocks;
think of granite veined with pale-rose quartz,
a fret of stone where the bracken's frayed
by aching, flint-pierced, moorland streams;
the bind of ivy, the prick of gorse,
hedged in with comfrey, helleborine;
sob of rain, scar of hail, snow shrinking
to sigh, the sound of words you can't say.

Cancel the Invite II
(9/8: NIGHT)

(from Plato, via Eliot)

If you came, if you came this way to our city,
taking the old road, the salt road, up from the harbour,
and it's early days, mid-morning, late September,
sky an upturned limpet's shell, flesh-scooped, chalk blue –
or later, maybe, at dusk in depths of winter,
the sky a pebble dropping to a shore-line pool;
and if you came, if you should slip through our gates
while our guards are down, dealing out their final hands –
Proteus back from exile to walk our boarded streets,
beggar, broken king, virgin trembling on the brink
(for we know you can change face – and heart – at will);
and if you reached, by chance, our marbled market halls
to find some unclaimed spot, set out your same old wares
we've all seen, we've all heard too many times before
(and besides could buy cheaper in our local stores),
then we'd welcome you as a stranger, as a guest,
wash your dusty feet, throw fresh garlands round your neck,
commend your art, revere your turncoat trickster's skill,
and then, because poets are forbidden here by law –
for we need doctors, surgeons, men to find the cure –
we'd show you, so politely, to the waiting door.

Set it in Stone
(13/8)

I
A new green shoot
                    your strong, deep root
but still I withered on the stalk
my mother thought me flawless
my family prayed for rain
            five summers –
                            and then earth again

(Egypt, c.300 CE)

II
The gods are jealous of those who love

I can't touch you now, Posilla
my words are stone
            my heart a fist against grey rock

(Italy, c.100 BCE)

III
a seven year flowering
and now I'm going back to bud

the rose you cut for me that morning –
yellow for my seedling hair –
blooms on above my ashen head
opens, closes, with each earth-bound eye
my sun, my stars, my stretch of fire-scorched sky

(Letchworth, 1996)

Demeter in Winter
(31/10)

And my grief is hardening, blade by blade,
with the grass. This month it's the raw white card
in newsagents' blurring windows: SMALL PRAM
WANTED or GIRL'S BIKE FOR SALE, JUST OUTGROWN:
it's the stray, stiff glove spiked on garden walls,
each child-chaired car iced over on its slot
in caring supermarket parking-lots,
songs slicing out like sleet through playground bars...

Centuries on and I can wake believing
that nothing's changed, that she's still here sleeping
in the room next door. Then I have to know
again how I could lose her, cell by cell,
how she could slip away, how she could fade –
that first, uncertain fall of rain-washed snow.

In Coventry
(22/12)

Even the angels are refugees,
etched in pain between past
and present, the world they have
and the one they want but just can't reach.
And here I am, in Gethsemane,
caught between Piper's Light
and Sutherland's soul-dark shrine,
an agnostic, a confirmed apostate,
lighting candles for the freshly dead;
a press-gang pilgrim with a Janus face
whose own faith blew out years ago,
still waiting on a miracle, a sign,
I know, I'm sure, will never show.

So now, of course, along it comes:
a group of school-kids gusting in
like shattered glass or keening wind
swept up the nave in threes or fours,
each hand a bead without the wood,
the rosary scraps we used to link –
about her age at final count,
the age we sisters must've been
on that first family expedition;
in matching coats and pinafores,
shrugging off their grown-up dreams
with our strange games and jointed speech,
our own dolls-house religion.

Which when I need I can't have back
and won't believe: *To The Glory
Of God This Cathedral Burned*:
one more grudge to hold against Him –
or try the light-charged vanity of man
who'll burn it down to build it up,
thousands squandered for the spectacle,
yet from my fallen, worm's-eye view,

it's just this one death I can't take.
Still I've not come for absolution,
but to curse the hand that could make
her cells divide, multiply
and stop ours from reproducing...

I know she'll never speak to us again
but today I saw her last face
in the face of a ravaged angel. And this
is where it starts and where it ends:
grief, fear, blame – the purging flames
of loss and gain. Reconciliation.

from Heroics

Fresh Meat: *a perversion of* Iliad, *22*

That day he dazzled like the Dog Star on a moonless sky,
rising in the dark as summer fades – too bright for bare eyes,
a fever surging through my veins, the old, old delusion:
that yes, we must die, but not now, not yet.
                                         The old man said
I was going to the dogs, leaving him to be butchered
by the wild curs of Greece, to lie rotting, spat at, savaged
by the very hounds who now licked crumbs from his upturned palms.
But by then I would've taken Lord Achilles in my arms,
stripped the bronze from his oiled body to whisper in his ear:
'Forget Helen. Forget your dark ships lying at anchor
in my deep seas. Forget this grey city which will haunt us
for all time; its ghosts are old already and we're too young –
far too young – to tread their ashen paths.'
                                        But we were warriors
not lovers lying side by side in hazy summer fields,
talking out our lives as dandelion or parsley seed
drifted down in search of former flower. And I knew – I knew
he would have killed me where I stood, naked and trembling, trapped
like a woman, when I had shed the armour from my skin;
for us, after Patroclus, there could be no forgetting
and no forgiveness, no friendship, no faith, no trysts, no trust,
until we'd slaked our blood-lust, repaid with increased interest
the high-rate sorrow of love long lost…
                                  As he raised his spear,
I saw at once the evening star caught above the coves
where I had fished as a boy, that first shaft of light falling
on the mackerel scaled and gutted in our boats, floating
down the waters like a sail unfurled from a black, black ship.
And I watched him as he scoured my skin for that one soft spot
where the flesh might best be pierced; as he found it on my neck
between jugular and wind-pipe, and then drove home the point,
leaving me just breath enough to beg for more. Although now
it was my lord who turned to me and spoke at last:

'You thought
that if you killed Patroclus you would finally be safe.
Hector, couldn't you remember that I was his shield-arm,
his spear-fist, his sword-hand, his eyes, his lips, his beating heart,
the lungs through which he still breathed? How could you forget, you fool,
that another man would be watching, waiting, in the ships,
a stronger man, a swifter man, a man who would bring you
to your knees? Or did you think you could escape the full force
of my fury? Now the dogs and crows will tear your heart out;
mine will be buried with Patroclus.'
                                        But still I pleaded
on my life, on my knees, by all the love he had once known,
not to leave me there for the strays from the ships to savage.
And I offered him my body weighed out in bronze and gold.
'How dare you,' he snarled back, 'speak to me of barter, of love?
For if I had the strength, if I could but find the stomach,
I would slice you into pieces and feed on you myself
for the hurt you've done to me. And even if you brought me
ten times your body weight in bronze, paid bone for bone in gold,
only dogs will have the pleasure of your flesh.'
                                        'As you wish,'
I told him as I fell. 'Since I know you too well – a heart
hammered from raw iron. But believe me, my lord, your turn,
too, will come; already the jealous gods plot against you
and death waits like a lover at the Gates. For just one cell
of mortality will suffice, dividing in secret
as you sleep, the cancer creeping through your marrow – just one
slim ankle-joint, believe me, the tiniest shard of bone,
can end it all. One small robber cell waiting in the dark
to betray you without pity, without cause…
                                        …Achilles,
the stars will still be shining, the dark seas will turn and turn,
but not for us, as other men claim their share of the light;
our flesh won't return to the bone. This virus won't retreat.

My friend, your time will come.
                                And I will meet you in the ash.'

from Odyssey

Scilly

This time we've gone too far,
disturbed the balance of our minds.
We start to fight for spit and bar,
dodge the draft, abandon mines.

We ride the swell with dipping hearts,
cling to monoliths like masts;
we sweat spray, we speak frets,
breathe in sea, piss out wrecks.

By day our tales swim off the page,
tongues crust up with salt and blood.

At night we dream of brick and clay,
sunken lanes caked in mud.

Easter in Sancreed

The talk is of home, our small histories,
tales we tell to shore up our shifting pasts:
old jokes, old gibes, the same old childhood roles –
the one who strayed but never seemed to go.
Mist slinks across the bay, the Mount recedes,
and in the Rowes slumped back against the lych,
we stumble on some greater, graver piece:
my great-grandparents' great-grandparents

we must have brushed past time and time again
without seeing them, without sensing us.
We sponge the splintered slab with rain-soaked moss,
scrape back ivy, chisel clinging lichen,
retrace their path from porch to font to rail
then back outside once more to waiting soil.
And in the grass at last I have to understand:
even here, even now, you're slipping from my hands.

Letchworth Crematorium

                              I dug my own hole:
sword-scraped the pit, an elbow's breadth,
poured libations to the world below –
milk first, mixed with honey, then fine wine,
clear water; I sowed seeds, daily bread,
got down on my knees and begged the dead,
promised I would sacrifice it all,
pile my worldly goods on pyres, scald shrines
with entrails of my flocks, my best head –
one black sheep, two barren cows, more ewes –
whatever they wanted from my marble halls.
And then, when I'd paid my Hades dues,
I slit a throat, watched life blood flow out,
dark clouds moving across dusk-dyed skies.
Now they came from the pit on each side,
souls of the dead, souls of the dying
with heart-stop cry. And my fear was green
like creeping mould, damp, knotted, gnawing:
soldiers, battle-slain and battle-stained,
brides, bachelors, long-suffering old men
and girls, seedling shoots, fresh for mourning.

Return to Ithaca (via Cavafy)

(Without her, you would never have set sail.
But she has nothing left to show you now…)

I can't believe the journey holds the key,
only the arriving, the death of need:

a mother tortured by those lightning nights,
father planting out his grief to seed;
the wife whose heart unravels with the light,
each dog who's had its day: they mark your map.

And then there's the land that can hold its own,
the groves whose darkness opens like a trap;
soil you'll feed with blood, mulch with lovers' bones,
furrows ploughed then filled, the blade's twist and theft.

These dreams still coil around you in the deep,
old songs returning ten-fold with the nets.
They wait there now: rooms you'd sack at a stroke –
the one place you will pollute to possess.

The Word for Sorrow

(2009)

Hail

A dismal spring, first of a new millennium
and three weeks (so far) of relentless rain;
lines are down, Perseus can't save the day,
no help now from latinvocabdotcom.
no hope but to return to the old addiction.
I slide the book down softly from the shelf,
dustier now, with that tell-tale whiff of rot.
Sudden hail taps on the window pane –
impatient late collection, rattled box,
slap of spade on long-buried inscription –

and there, as if still fresh, on the front page,
dual initials, double-barrelled surname:
G. A. Lyneham-Forsythe, 6th January 1900
scrawled in schoolboy boredom, thunder-stiff,
blood-brown ink, faint as an old man's vein:
the bruising flare of chained sheet lightning
that flashes, strikes, then moves on
                    leaving everything changed.

Naso All at Sea

sparks glitter, cloud to cloud
        thunder clatters, Jove-loud

We're lifted up, up, to touch the stars,
plunged down, down, into Hell's black jaws,
pitched into abyss as each swell sinks
(spray stops my lips as I speak, write this).
Look around: sky and sea, sea and sky,
the one flecked white, other furrowed grey;
gales rage between, god-forsaken, fierce,
uncertain which element to serve.
I don't fear death just the way it comes –
save me now and death would be welcome.
For if sea should subside, storm be lulled –
if I live on, I live in exile.
So why – *why?* – wish for propitious winds?
In Sarmatia this trail must end.
I pray for safe landing, far from home,
sigh that this road to hell seems too slow;
strive for Tomis, last stop of the world,
that Black Sea, ice-hard, hail-stiff, snow-whirled;
plead for my safe passage – to Tomis!

in searching out light
        I'm staring at darkness

Dancing in the Dark

For days now I've been stumbling after,
chasing down words just beyond reach,
searching for agreement, unpicking order,
trying not to tread on toes (or feet)

to keep up, as ever, with his deft repartee:
Writing poems that no one will read,
Naso sighed, *is like dancing in the dark,*
the gesture no one sees you make –

shame I can't find it in this stiff dictionary.
Light shrinks. Ashen stars graze the Ghyll.
A half-moon teeters on to dusk-scraped sky;
Orion traced, tip-toeing into place –

the hour for logging off and standing by,
last minute searches, last chance Googles,
as lines reel down to score its faint initials
but now a Proper name, new place, new date:

Geoffrey, April, Nineteen Fifteen,
Gloucester Yeomanry off to Gallipoli
(school Latin forgotten, for now, at least),
those same shadowed steps to the East.

Malvern Road Station, Cheltenham

I. APRIL 1915

For once let's not dwell on impending death,
scan the thumbs-up rows of grinning faces
like bone-starved worms grubbing out fresh flesh
for those who got thumbs down, didn't make it –
Wilf Barton, Tom Honey, first from the ship,
returned as cap, belt, identity disc –
a merry bunch, pleased as punch to be off,
that day of fête then cheerful letters home,
spry postcards from a holiday gone wrong:
the men and I drink weak tea now, talk Gloucs,
bullets seem like shrill birds at dawn chorus…
But back on the platform, between the smiles,
I spy Geoffrey, hesitant, stiff, crowd-shy,
already out with the burying party.

II. FEBRUARY 2005

I'd hoped for a single snowdrop hunched by the tracks –
Catullus' flower untouched, as yet, in the grass –
a star-chipped bloom to soothe the scar of waste,
stench of rot, almost sweet, smear of industrial estate.
But there's no hope, no art that can heal the past;
walls have been levelled, diggers come and gone.

The day fails, sky drags with unfallen snow;
the hour, already, of the plough and of the crow.
All we can do here is say nothing and move on.

Landed
I never knew blood smelt so strong…

For a prize of dirt, few square yards of scrub,
they fought like gods as soil soaked red,
shallows curdled, stagnant with corpse-shoals.

Across Suvla plain, Geoffrey's men marched out,
without maps, with no idea where to attack,
a storm-spray of chalk and dust and blood –

too dense, too dark to tell if theirs or ours.
They crawled back like ghosts, skin singed,
clothes in tatters, tongues burnt black,

press-ganged workers after abattoir nightshift;
some spoke only in whimpers, others cried
for comrades mown down by unseen scythe,

smouldering khaki all that marked the spot.
Now the dried salt lake brimmed with body parts
as if netted by fishermen's bumper catch:

Englishmen. Dead Englishmen. Hundreds of them.
We'd never seen a corpse before and here they were,
stacked like logs or mackerel on moon-blanched shore,

mouths open, eyes wide, all just staring back,
our horror reflected in each gasping, glassy face.
We thought of home. It seemed a happy place.

Between the Lines

It seems so snug here in my grave –
you can't describe it any other way:
two feet deep, piled up with earth,
cracked headstone to protect us,
a few rancid scraps of wood,
sea-salvage, to line the box,
my mackintosh on sticks for lid
(last night a five-inch centipede
decided to share my valise –
I soon made short work of it!).
Shells rattle, universe shattered,
but so far not too much damage –
one chap had his trousers blown off –
after a few hours one takes no notice.
No flies yet, well, at least, we hope
maybe because rations are so tight:
lime juice daily, tot of rum at night.
We've had a lesson in bomb-throwing
and now I am dying to have a go.
But one of us has to stay behind –
I tossed with Major Gething, lost.
The night was extraordinary, flames
soaring above the horizon like lightning
leap-frogging across stormy Wolds;
the fires of a hundred Cerney carnivals
searing the landscape, whole world lit up.
All I could do was stand and watch.
Gething killed. Wilf Barton killed.
Gething! I tossed with him and lost.
My poor Sergeant Honey dead.
I must say I feel sad about that –
so many who came from home with us.
Today we had a go back at the Turks.
Good show: I hit my bag the last two shots.
I wish you were here to see the lights.
Funny, I feel I've been under fire all my life.

Naso Writes His Own Epitaph

If on this page you detect some new hand, fresh script
I have dictated, don't fret: for I am sick –
sick, here at the end of the unknown world, half-dead
(reports of recovery exaggerated).
Here there's no rest-home, rations fit for invalid,
no one with physician's skill in pain relief;
no one to comfort, wile away convalescence
with tall tales, no friend to sit in attendance.
Stranded far away, thoughts of home creep up in vain
but most of you, dear wife, so I mouth your name,
whisper at shades, sigh at shadows: they take your shape.
Night falls, day breaks, thoughts of you a deep dull ache.
But defer grief, dear wife, until my bones are home,
find them some suburban plot, out-of-town tomb.
And for the eyes of travellers hurrying past,
carve these letters on marble sarcophagus:
HERE LIES A PLAYER: IN LIFE, IN LOVE, IN TENDERNESS –
NASO, THE POET, DESTROYED BY HIS GENIUS.
LOVERS, PASS BY, PASS BY. I PRAY YOU WON'T BEGRUDGE ME
THIS LAST REQUEST: ON NASO'S BONES TREAD SOFTLY.
Such inscription will suffice. For my books will
prove a greater, a more lasting memorial.
In these I put my trust, despite their treachery –
to restore my good name for eternity.
Still we should give the dead their due, fair offerings:
wreaths moist with tears, monuments to suffering.
For if fire consumes, condemns flesh and bone to ash,
dust remembers. It hears our step, craves our touch…

Among the Graves: Green Hill, Gallipoli

By a broken sign down an unmarked track,
just wide enough for horse and cart to pass,
there is a hushed grove for hollow graves.
An open-air cathedral arched by pine,
four fattened cedars as sacrificial altar,
memorial slabs lined round in pews;
a stub of stones, milk teeth, broken through
for the half-formed fighting men they sowed.
Thy Glory Shall Not Be Blotted Out
claims Tom Honey's mossed inscription.
Remembered with Honour insists Gething's.
For Wilf Barton *Thy Will be Done* –
off-the-peg words from those who never came,
pattern-book blooms, chrysanthemums, aster,
perennial guardians for bone-bare tombs;
two thousand five hundred and eighty-nine
long-broken bodies that have never been found.

Back by the gate, a lone stork takes flight,
marbled butterflies brush past, 'half-mourners',
insistent, impatient to shed black for white.
I wish now I'd spoken out, roll-called the names,
taken one small thing, at least, home to Gloucs:
rosemary sprig to dry, daisy or phlox to press
between **calamitas**. *hurt* and *healed*. **consanatus.**

Last Orders

It should be our feast day at home, village fête –
the street all lit up, stalls set out, but instead
we're pulling ticks from shirts, waiting for first shot…

I've been walking too long in the paths of the dead
like trench fly cooling my feet in their icy tracks –
even here, in Gloucs, my car trails a slick of blood

on frost-flayed lanes, dictionary swapped for map
and faded handbill: RECRUITS WANTED AT ONCE.
(MEN TO HAVE THE OPTION OF FOREIGN SERVICE):

'26 joined' scored across in flowery pencil,
pulling men not pints: Kings Head, Elliott Arms, Cerney –
lads that had known each other since the cradle

too eager to share the next stage of their journey.
Today I sip coffee in those same, morning-sad bars;
heads shake, shoulders shrug, but there's no sign,

no last orders for 26 lost and home-sick ghosts.
By The Bull at Fairford, old boys in buttoned coats
and checked ties debate Afters: *custard or ice cream?* –

Wilf Barton if he'd lived, Alf Honey, Hugh Gething.
Out in the sleet-blurred square, a black van slows,
flesh for freight; back doors slide open, rattle

as the butcher steps out in blooded apron, slings a pig's
half carcass across his shoulder. Stops. Then gently shifts
the weight as if carrying a comrade from battle.

Dictionary Definitions

Construct the landscape of slaughter:
lakes, hills, forts, flesh-clogged river.
The Rhine, too, fractured, splintered,
dammed with bodies and running red
with its own blood . . .

My job now to distinguish **caedes** from **cruor**;
the one *carnage, slaughter, a battle massacre*
and the other simply *blood, that which flows*
from the wound. And then there's **lugubria**
– almost comic in English – but solemn here,
of or belonging to mourning, and in the plural,
substantive, *mourning clothes, weeds for widows.*

This shroud of Latin: **amissus. mortuus.**
The dragging, leaden cloak of language:
missing in action, presumed dead.

Naso Sees Action

Let me voice it: exile, soldier – said for respite not renown;
to stop the heart, free the thought by writing it down.
For my Muse travels with me, my friend, my betrayer,
and I am drawn to her like besotted lover.
I, whose name was on all lips, the toast of Rome,
must now defend my life, what must be my home.
Now I live among wild tribes: Getae, Sauromate –
no longer safe but entrenched by wall and gate.
In youth I shunned the rigours of military service
never took up arms unless in play or at the Circus.
In my old age now I must strap on sword and shield
as my trembling hands take cold comfort of steel;
as soon as the signal sounds, shout from watch-turret,
on a greying head of hair I buckle helmet.
Our fierce enemy brandish arrows dipped in venom,
encircle the walls with snorting horse, breath frozen.
Should we dare to leave our ramparts, venture out alone,
they fall on us like wolves on sheep outside the fold.
So this is now my home, a new landscape of fear;
for all time, it seems (and more), fate has shipped me here.
And if my Muse still dances to those same old tunes,
I write for myself, read to myself: what else can I do?
To whom can I recite my verse? Who knows the steps?
Who can hear the music, follow Latin syntax?
Yet my work, at least, is safe in my own judgment –
for those who cannot read can give no assessment.
Many lines are inscribed although most are condemned –
still I send them home in the hope you will read them.

Welcome Note

At last there is a link, a line, a letter:

I have to admit that I've been better;
I feel like a rag, seedy from dysentery,
prescribed soup, Bovril – and champagne,
half a bottle, which had me half-drunk, dizzy.
But bread and butter was the greatest treat –
marvellous after hard biscuits and bully beef.
Still, men go to hospital and are never seen again;
it's a poisonous place, very full, not well run . . .

On the ship we're stacked, rotten fruit in crates,
each day the dead cleared overboard for space
to swim beside us, bandages trailed like plankton.
A lad by me, head bound, lily-pale, raved for hours,
waving his tarnished trench trowel: 'Kill the bastards!'
before swivelling round to beg a pencil from us.
We thought he wanted to scribble a last note home
but he used it for lever to ease his dressing,
gore dripping down his face in baptismal blessing.

At Alexandria they gave us clean sheets, pyjamas,
the first since landing, a lifetime ago, at Suvla.
I looked in the mirror and hardly knew myself:
an old man looking back, black hair bleached
to white. I thought of the swans by the church,
wings unfolding like ancient maps or manuscripts.
Tonight the stars were half-murmured words
sliding softly into sound after far too long.

And then one of the women sang your song.

Seeking Quarter

I. NASO

Send new orders, please: if I can't go home
then a softer place of exile, a step nearer
but far enough away from these savage foes
who count our corpses as fair plunder.
As for those who revel in the killing –
fathers sending kids for slaughter,
gods thirsting for blood-drenched altars,
sons or brothers driven by their own Furies –
they don't know it yet but they are caught here
beneath these ice-veined skies, living
under the same fallen stars as me…

II. GEOFFREY

For the sick of heart – or stomach –
there can be no reprieve, no respite;
a few weeks, maybe months, to recuperate
and then straight back to the fight.
For nurses, sheets, Geoffrey must pay penance,
blood-price: hurt for healing, bone for bone.
On a frost-edged November night, crescent
moon blown through the sky like bullet-hole,
the Turks hurled a note into the trench:
We can't advance, you can't advance.
What can anyone achieve? Where to go?

Among the Graves: Salonica

Lives shrunk to map, War Graves certificate
and blurred snap of a summer's day in Greece.
On a slab by the planes, far out of sight,
I'd find my father's name: Edward Balmer,
April 1918, just months from home:
my grandmother never really recovered,
in her grief she gave a guinea to those
prepared to name their first-born son for hers;
shout 'Ted' in our street, a League team answered...
(and in time, of course, it would have been mine
– if not for this lack of Y chromosome).
Above the trees a nimbus noses east,
on the grass beneath, shadows like flayed skins
ward away ghosts: the dead locked out. And in.

Naso the Barbarian

I see a world without culture, savage, bleak,
a world weighed by sorrow. So men become beasts
with no fear of Law; Justice vanquished in war.
Learning, commerce, tainted now by Getic burr.
My own voice is spent, this poet's coinage,
my native speech bankrupted, impoverished.
So I talk to myself, deal in borrowed words
for this doomed art, the currency of my verse.

And then, watching the tribesmen in the markets,
bartering for goods in their common language,
while I communicate by mime or gesture,
a thought occurs: who is the barbarian here?

The Penny Pot

And still the ghosts come back to haunt us:
you know he served twice, my grandfather,
he went back again after it was all over –

well, the marriage wasn't going so good –
to dig out the dead, a rest from the pits,
and identify the corpses, where he could.

A strong man, a skater, champion runner,
his house in Thatto Heath full of memorabilia:
spurs, knives, guns, a cartridged bandolier.

And this. For as long as I can remember
it has stood on my father's study book-case,
offering spare change for flag-wavers

and poppy-sellers, rattled collection boxes;
paper-clips, pins, tiny keys for lost valises.
Three-legged, slightly tilted, tarnished,

forged, so I'd thought, at school metal class,
boys practising before coal or glass.
Today, as I take it, inhale its stale burnish,

I can see that its cup is a spent shell-head,
and for its triple legs, three bullets sharp
as memory, pennies saved for Charon's fare;

the known, our omphalos, suddenly unfamiliar –
a Sibyl's tripod suspended in miniature
deciphering its sulphur dreams in the dark.

The Word for Sorrow

On the fly leaf I've written
my new date, my own name:
Josephine Balmer, January 6th 2005
Do we find a text or does it find us?

Two brothers caged in eastern prison,
unable to stand, cramped in darkness,
passed the years by crossing Paris
in their mind's eye: arrondissement
by arrondissement. One would pick
two points, the other would trace
the way between – a city they had visited
only on crumpled map, by fingertip.
A path they had never taken.
A path they would always tread.

Does it matter if the journey exists
only in a captive's imagination
or the arch of a writer's eyebrow?
If Naso tricked us, never left Rome;
if 'Geoffrey's' story isn't all his own?
And would I like them if we'd met:
the player-poet with an ego even
greater than his sense of grievance?

Or retired Major, double-barrelled,
Master of the Hunt, local magistrate,
for whom Latin meant status, gender,
but never learning, love, literature?
And when the old order disappeared,
let it go for the rest of us to scavenge –
the mark of power for two millennia –
leaving our speech forever scarred,
like the taint of Naso's barbarian burr,
no going back, known world changed.

And how to tell if these shades I summon
thank or curse me, condone or condemn?
If this new life isn't a new death;
if they'd hate this fresh shroud of flesh,
fret, like harbour-bound trawlermen,
for the heart-stop stench of gutted bone?

Yet once in the cemetery at Marazion
as darkness fell, a priest, a surgeon
to heal the fractured Bay, make it whole,
I sensed two figures, unseen ghosts
at each shoulder, as if my ancestors
had risen from the grave at which
I'd just picked out a weed like editor
adjective or politician, statistic:
the house-maid and the labourer,
guiding my path between fallen stars
before language, semantics, divide us.

I know my words are not their words,
I know my thoughts are not their thoughts
but every past must have a present.
And their cells are now my cells
and their matter is now my matter:
sometimes rain-hewn granite, the gorse
curved, carved by moorland squalls;
sometimes ore-bled river, forged course
from Kenidjack to Cape Cornwall.

And today in Sussex it's the drizzled gulls,
risen, flagged, like a sudden thought,
from Ghyll to Weald to Down,
where ancestors aren't flesh and bone
but the musty chatter and tented laughter
of a summer's day at a hospital fête:
all those months waiting for life to begin,
a restless Celt in the land of Saxon, Latin,
learning these new lines of dominion.

We none of us need a dictionary
to define the word for sorrow:
Tomis, Gallipoli, Salonica, name
upon name etched on empty graves;
date upon date end-stopped in one same year.
Or a plaque in a country cemetery
that can't even reach double figures,
Catullus' flower passed by the furrow…

We are all translating the same story
search same words in same thesaurus.
What drives us on, keeps us to our path,
in every version is not gain but loss.

The Paths of Survival

(2017)

Proem: Final Sentence
(Bodleian Library, Oxford, Present Day)

Still I am drawn to it like breath to glass.
That ache of absence, wrench of nothingness,
stark lacunae we all must someday face.

I imagine its letters freshly seared;
a scribe sighing over ebbing taper,
impatient to earn night's coming pleasures
as light seeped out of Alexandria.

But in these hushed corners of Oxford
Library afternoons, milky with dust,
the air is weighted down by accruing loss

and this displaced scrap of frayed papyrus
whose mutilated words can just be read,
one final, half-sentence: *Into darkness…*
Prophetic. Patient. Hanging by a thread.

from Custodians

The Librarians' Power
(The National Library, Baghdad, 2003)

We carried what we could to safety.

They seemed like something living:
fungus on an oak, the pleated folds
of open mushroom cup, organisms
that were once books, manuscripts,
now debris of 'precision' incendiary.

To conserve them we needed ice
not fire. In a ruined kitchen cellar
we found a freezer but no power;
we canvassed, coaxed, cajoled
until locals offered the sacrifice
of their one precious generator.

We were asked why we struggled
to save books while all around us
so many of our citizens were lost.
We could only say that, if not flesh,
here were dividing cells, bare blocks
of collective memory. Conscience.

The vast record of all our knowledge
and of our faith: an ancient Quran,
the House of Wisdom we had built;
the learning we alone had salvaged
and then protected for the Greeks –
Ptolemy's *Almagest*, science, medicine.

Those lost worlds were retrieved
in the flash of forceps, lifting piece
on tiny piece, word on broken word.
Our own enduring, unshakeable belief

that in each newly-deciphered letter
a poem waited to be recovered.

from Excavators

The Student's Find
(Oxyrhynchus, Egypt, 1932)

I was only too happy to keep
my head down, hands in muck
and silt. At home in Florence,
we were pinkos, pederasts,
as the thugs waited on street
corners, ready to smash fists
in faces, ribs – or worse…
Even a former *carabiniere*
had been arrested, we heard,
sentenced to five years' *confino*,
ditto the boy he had adored –
filth, infections to be purged.

I signed up for the Institute dig
as my fellow students teased –
the most fastidious of our party
shovelling shit on his knees.
Now I watch our stout spiv
of a site director puffing past,
spotless, in his shiny spats
and striped suit, trilby cocked,
dressed for dinner not detritus.
Still, he offers a way to live:
'Politics are not my business,'
he says, 'I care only for papyri.'

Sometimes as I sift the pieces
broken lives slot back into place –
shrill petitions, desperate pleas;
the constant, unremitting fear,
that makes us flatter, supplicate.
And then, like the first flicker
of smoking fire, slow to take,
I found a tattered word: *Antelexa.*

My heart turned over. I knew it:
speak out. oppose. dissent.

Later there came confirmation
from the professors in Florence;
I had unearthed a precious sliver
of Aeschylus' lost *Myrmidons* –
a new sigh from a long silence.
A stifled cry shuddering back:
Enough is enough. No more slander,
no more slurs to crush the tongue.
Time now to protest, to dissent.

A point of no return. The moment
all the lies might start to shatter.

from Editors

Redaction
(John Cramer, The Royal Library, Paris, July 1834)

I barely saw the city. I tracked down
only texts for extract. But as I studied,
the Library's high windows shuddered
with the shouts of rioters – republicans,
radicals, they told us. On Rue Vivienne
the injured were stowed like receipted
books or consulted papers. One corpse
lay crumpled, a read note, in the street.
I walked on by, non-aligned. I thought
of the desk I had just left, its volumes
still untouched, smooth as fresh sheets.

Yet even here I was no longer safe.
As the hiss and boom of gunfire ceased,
I turned a leaf, easing out the crease,
leaning on my elbows for weight;
an old manuscript, deep in the collection,
a work I should never have breached:
I am absolved because I loved him –
a reference, if I was not much mistaken,
to the unspeakable vice of the Greeks.
In Aeschylus! I copied author and play
then scratched them out. Better not to say.

from Scavengers

The Clerk's Crusade
(Constantinople, 12th April 1204)

The first thing we noticed was mortar
crumbling, sand trickling from a stone.
Even rats, the Captain shrugged, get restless
under siege, gnawed by our same hunger.
The guards returned to their next throw
of dice. And I slunk back to Library desk.

We could not know, did not even guess
our city was already falling, already ash.

Next day we all saw it, the slab shift
and slowly tilt. We stood transfixed
as a single block of wall rolled back
and chasm opened where it collapsed;
ten withered fingers gripped the edge,
then Crusader helmet on Crusader head.
Our captain gave orders. On cue we fled.

That night Byzantium was melted down.
Everything they could move, they took.
All else was toppled into steaming pots,
vast statues shrunk to stumps of bronze,
for each piece of tessera, another life lost.

Myself, I looted what they overlooked.

As Latin bishops stripped our churches
of jewels, I stuffed my splattered jerkin
with a few foxed and battered books:
Photius' *Lexicon*, Lucian, Athenaeus.
Here was no Holy War but Christian
against Christian, West against East.
Better the Saracens. They had belief.

I ran back through the streets, slipping
on spilt blood, fresh excrement, filth.
Far off, a woman sobbed, out of reach.
I squeezed out through the breach,
a conqueror in reverse. For in Nicaea
or the monasteries of Thessalonica,
we would soon found another empire.
Our nobles crept away like thieves
as the Latins jeered, waving inkpots,
quills – the weapons not of warriors
but meek scholars, they hissed.

                              Let them mock.

Where they had cruelty, we had culture.
Where they had greed, we had Greek.

from Translators

Gerard's Constellations
(Southern Spain, 1175)

I came to Toledo to map the stars.

I was hunting Ptolemy's *Almagest*,
the key to our crammed skies, held safe
there all these centuries by the Moors.
Its charts, I heard, steered men homewards
through ink-black seas, night's vastness,
constellations tracked as if by a thread.

Now I saw it all, sphere on sphere
worlds opening up, unlocked doors –
catalogued, fixed, holding us here.

After the skies I discovered the earth:
medicine, mathematics, the healing works
of the Greeks, studded with metaphor,
a science that glittered like poetry.

So I translated them, last in a chain –
Greek to Arabic and now my Latin –
striving to be faithful yet make them sing.

But alone at night I found myself dreaming
of other, unknown poets; the anguish
of their words drifting out into darkness,
as if sailors becalmed by unfamiliar waters
with no way back when the daylight falters.
And, in cloud, stars are slowly extinguished,
dimming, one by one, before they vanish.

from Victors

Amr's Last Words
(Fustat, Egypt, 664)

That night earth crept close to heaven
and I was crushed between, breathing
in through eye of a needle, unafraid
now, the stilled voice of a dying man.
Around my tented couch, the deserts
I had subdued stretched out, oblivious;
stars inked new scripts on dulled skies
as my life shrunk to sand speck, dust.
I remembered Alexandria, possessing
a city of 4,000 palaces & 4,000 baths,
400 marble theatres, 200 greengrocers
& 1 Library. I heard how the Ptolemies
filled the shelves with borrowed books,
confiscated 'tax' from anchored ships,
instructing their scribes to copy works
in secret, returning only the duplicates.
I had to choose which to save and which
to burn. Those that spoke of God I kept,
the rest, as ordered, went in the furnace.

The tragedies of the Greeks were first.
I can hear the crack of curled papyrus,
still smell that acrid, smouldering ash.

You ask what death tastes like. It is this.

from Believers

The Christians' Cheek
(Alexandria, 391)

We're old hands these days,
true believers for decades –
apart, of course, for the break
effected by Julian the Apostate
(when we found it was politic
to revert – just for the interim –
to blood rites, full sacrifice).
Now we've changed back again.

Our new emperor Theodosius
has outlawed all pagan practice,
that tribe of soothsayers, seers;
all the priests of Thoth, Serapis,
trite dramatists, epigrammatists
with their sharp-tongued sneers.
We'll storm their prized Libraries,
strip the dwindling shelves bare.
Who needs poetry or philosophy
when you have faith, orthodoxy?

For we are so tired of turning
the other cheek; time to shed ink,
shred parchment. It's a while since
we've put a knife to fine calf-skin.

from Anthologists

Erotic Tales
(Lucian, Samosata, Syria, 200)

I'd thought of myself as the new Homer.

But readers, I soon learnt, prefer horror,
sci-fi. My *Erotic Tales* pay the bills,
bring in the hard cash, the boys and/or girls.
Even Aeschylus, known for weighty verse,
dipped his nib in the ambidextrous:
such sacred communion between the thighs
sighed his Achilles over pert backside
to top my list of things bi-curious.

And who's to say I'm not as lyrical?
Across the empire, at any scribe's stall,
my 'lightweight' prose is still copied ten times
more than dull, turgid tragedies. Is this
a talent wasted? Or career waylaid?
Weighty or not, they'll remember my lines
when Aeschylus' plays have long decayed.

from Scribe

Blot
(Alexandria, 150)

It barely matters if I blot or blotch –
these days no one asks for Aeschylus.

As light fades I head for the streets –
a cheap tavern or the house of whores –
to scrub off this stain of guilt and remorse,
flaws that cling like yesterday's rotten fish.
On mornings after, I retake my seat,
propping up each eyelid with stylus tip,
making errors I can later edit…

And then today, a buyer for my script –
some pompous provincial bureaucrat
up from Oxyrhynchus with cold, hard cash
(although he couldn't tell drama from dog shit
all he cares is how it looks on the shelf).

For him I etch these words of love and grief.
I think of my wife, dead after a few weeks;
there'd been a baby, some complication,
the pockmarked physician couldn't tell which.
I came back one night and she was gone.

Into darkness… The skin I, too, must live in.
Mistakes uncorrected, holding the blame.

The only words left now to mask the pain.

from Annotators

Margin
(Didymus 'Chalcenterus', Alexandria, 20 BCE)

In this line of work
you have to make
things small, short.
So I digest the refs,
pin down each taut
twist of grammar
or some rare idiom,
poetry's last crumbs -
swallow them whole
(it's not for nothing
I'm called 'Iron-guts')
then spit them all out.
Well, all except jokes.
Now I have to decipher
the so-called 'comedies'
of vulgar Aristophanes.
It's no laughing matter:
you need to annotate
every last, single letter –
the text is crude, obscure.
Still I am never sure
what's quite so jocular.
My fellow Scholiasts
try to help, to translate:
they point out puns
and double entendres.
See, they say, a tragic
chorus of Aeschylus
has become a comic
ditty, satirical rhyme.
Just call it: 'parody'.
Parody. Hmm. Poor
imitation you'll find,
the desperate remedy
of the uninspired, bereft
of anything else left
to say for themselves.
And then yesterday

a few colleagues read
a 'new' commentary
they said they'd found
for me. Immediately
I disagreed on almost
every point. They said
nothing just sniggered
behind their hands –
until they confessed
the points were mine,
all cobbled together
from my own footnotes.
I had a new name:
'Forget-What-Wrote'.
If that was a joke
I still didn't get it.
For here on the edge,
I said, there's always
a margin of error.
That just made them
laugh even more.
Aristophanes has
a lot to answer for.

from Bureaucrats

The Ferryman's Roll
(Alexandria, c.245 BCE)

The lads tease me, call me Charon. I row
out to anchored ships at night, take my tax
as ferryman, not of pennies but texts,
as our Law decrees, seizing poems, plays
for transcribing in our new Musaeum,
swearing to return all works I 'borrow'.

Last week I took some rolls of Aeschylus
to Callimachus our famed Librarian:
gilt horse-cockerel mastheads, we read, perplexed,
crafted with care, are melting, drip by drip,
in the corrosive fires of burning ships…
We joked how they must drink, these Athenians.

Callimachus did not laugh. It was fate
he said: here were the Greek prows at Troy, torched
as Achilles sulked. *Myrmidons*. Lines thought
so precious that he would not give them back.
We all groaned, aghast. Not more horse-cocks.

And then I glanced at Callimachus's face
caught in a shifting taper as he talked –
like a city put to flame, molten wax
about to twist the world into new shapes.

from Copyists

Aeschylus' Desk
(Sicily, 370 BCE)

That summer we posed as his heirs, brothers
fallen on hard times, hawking salvaged flotsam
as the dramatist's 'desk', still scored, so we said,
with those wild, strange words – the language
of an unknown world. This tyrant, this Dionysius,
dripping in gold and cruelty, misplaced aspiration,
bought it at once for his new Temple of the Muses –
as if he could (as if!) become a poet by association.

We spent half our talents that night in a tavern,
drinking dark Sicilian wine, warm as blood.
The rest would keep us through the winter,
myself and my 'brother', my lover Sarpedon.
In those Syracuse mornings we wrote together,
bold new verse to surpass even the Athenians.
The nights – ah, the nights were for pleasure;
I can see his reed-thin body darting out of bed

to close the shutters against October showers,
falling back into my arms like a lightning flash,
his skin sharp as thyme, the tang of turquoise sea.
Yes, History would know our names at last:
Sarpedon of Rhegium and Diomedes of Gela.
As for Dionysius, he was never a player;
to tread these barbed paths, possess poetry,
you have to let go pride, relinquish power.

from Tragedian

Aeschylus' Revision
(Gela, Sicily, 456 BCE)

I have been trying to find a word
for the colour of the sea; wind-stirred
for days now, storm-faded, foam-
flecked, shadowed by the span of egret
wings, nosing north, heading home.
But it would take a lifetime to capture
and, as my Syrian physician concurs,
I have only a fraction of one left.
And Greek is too vague, the language
of the colour blind. *Chloros.* We use it
both of rain-drenched summer grass
and sun-blanched autumn straw ('Or piss,'
as the physician notes with relish).
If we Athenians ever need to evaluate,
variegate, differentiate, we must do it
by association, metaphor, epithet –
spray-whitened, blood-raged, death-dark –
the complex adjectives my critics
have long reviled for their strangeness;
the reason, perhaps, we are at heart
a nation of politicians, tricksters, poets,
trying to catch the fleeting, the imprecise
through our tongue's own imprecision,
those dark words scarring pale papyrus
but as we write a world bursts in to light.

* * * *

Back in Athens, I know, eyebrows
have been raised. There are murmurs
I have lost my reason with my soul,
the great democrat now among tyrants.
And I have to admit that when I found
'stipend: 10 talents' – I'm not proud –

etched across the dispatch from Gela,
another world moved into focus; vibrant,
vivid, not of fame or leisure or even luxury,
but more of space, time, opportunity.
Now I have come here not to create
but to revise, to rescore, to chisel away
the features of a life's work, scrape
off the layers of accumulated dust
from the shrivelled skin of my plays:
actors always want to build their part,
add in a line or two, make speeches longer;
chorus managers, the bankers, the money-
men, will try to dictate the course of art.
And then there is the lead weight
of public opinion, the sudden hush
of an audience as a play takes shape
or the muffled coughing, the shuffled feet,
when a line misfires or speech is fluffed,
the waiting dramatist, stone-struck, aware
of the slightest change in breath or beat,
fighting the urge to rewrite then and there
(in Athens we might live by committee
but not yet, thank Gods, compose poetry).
And slowly, stealthily, intricate threads
are dropped and a work's fragile integrity,
held as if a hesitant final breath, shatters
like a vase slipping from the hands
into a thousand, thousand fragments.

* * * *

I had planned to start with *Persians* –
my version of the war I'd helped to win
against barbarism, the death of civilisation.
But as the days shrink to my writing desk,
I find myself drawn now to *Myrmidons*,
the tragedy of pride, the tragedy of passion,
the heartbeat away we are from loss:
Achilles, the warrior who will not fight,
Patroclus, the lover he will sacrifice –

the one thing he needs to live, the cost
of those dried kisses, one small slight.
Who had to learn, like the rest of us,
that flesh never returns to the skeleton,
there is no coming back from Acheron…
I had not opened it for all these years –
the sharp taunts of its harshest critics
still sting, still reverberate in the ear.
They hated my tragic hero. Speechless
and veiled throughout its early scenes,
at first no actor would agree to play him.
I had to flatter, plead, bribe, cajole:
think of the shock, I begged, the thrill
when those first words finally ring out,
reverberate around the auditorium
like lightning, a sudden flash, sparking
from seat to seat, stone row to row.
(I reminded them how, at Marathon,
the order had come round to quiet us;
to stifle our battle cries as we ran
towards the Persians, to conserve
each last breath for the coming fight).
In those days I believed my work
could still cure our diseased world;
that words had the power to change
the old order. That I could write tyranny
into democracy, transform revenge
into justice, take away our every hurt.
That if you lost a love it could be found
between the creases of unrolled papyrus.
That each flaw could somehow salve itself,
providing someone paid the sacrifice.
But to create the healing I had
to create the horror too – the Furies
who would become the Eumenides,
the Kindly Ones; the bloodshed
that could be washed away, crimes
that could be atoned for. Now here it is,
unshrinking, indelible, for all time.

* * * *

If you lost a love… As I stare across
the bay, scything my way through faded
lines I had long given up on, stylus
sharper even than a hero's blade,
all I can see is another unvoiced colour –
another blurred *chloros*: a pair of eyes
turning to mine that day in the agora
we heard how those vast Persian armies
were now on their way to destroy us;
a young man's eyes, the eyes of a warrior
as pale and soft as the last few cornflowers
at the very end of summer. Cynaegirus.
'Find strength,' he said. 'Cities can fall
in the flash of a sword but faith, ideas,
take root like weeds in their shattered halls –
there is nothing now for us to fear.'
As Athens waited, all those months,
we shared one flesh, one skin, one breath.
When the storm came, we stood together
for those ten, never-ending August nights
at Marathon, life's blood, shield-brothers,
armed against the moment the fight
would finally begin. Now the piked plain
was indivisible from sea, shields glistening
like sun-dipped waves. Time was suspended,
a sigh exhaled, trapped like a feather
between the rounds of ocean boulders.
Later, stars clashed across the skies, Orion
leading the charge, bow strung, the Hunter.
Trapped beneath, I thought of Achilles,
of all those other young men at Troy
on another plain by another blooded sea,
who knew their lives might not be long.
At last the signal came to march, destroy;
Cynaegirus at my side, we reached the ships.
his eyes in mine in the heat of battle.
Yet I hesitated, felt my knees buckle,
as the fear that Homer coloured *chloros*
like stagnant water – dank, death-gripped –

took its clammy hold. Cynaegirus
did not falter. Smiling, he stepped up
to take my place. They said he fought
like a rabid beast: *when the enemy struck,*
on all sides like wolves scattering lambs,
who strapped his shield on slender arms
and single-handedly drove them home?
Who saved you? …And then he was gone,
flesh cut to pieces, life-thread cut short.
There is no coming back from Acheron…

* * * *

Afterwards, numb, I wrote *Myrmidons,*
never able to admit it was for him
struggling to give my Achilles words.
I thought I was moving through the years
letting my work dictate my life. Was it
always the other way round? The fears
that shadowed my youth are gone.
I am no longer concerned with the death
of the body only the death of the work.
My epitaph is written: *Here lies a man*
who fought at Marathon. My plays
will tell the rest, flesh-stripped bones.
A few weeks ago I dismissed the Syrian,
words now are my only physician,
from the horror comes the healing.
Poetry flourishes in the cracks of lies,
in the white spaces between the lines –
the place I dreamed my city into being
not of gold or marble but of iron Law,
where men must account for the killing.
Where *chloros* may be the colour of fear
but also of sky, sea, a pair of pale eyes.
I take out my stylus and begin to strike;
now I must emend, I must speak out,
acknowledge to myself, to the living
and to the dead, if they still care or listen:

my love, remember all the nights we shared.
What matters now is what survives;
what time corrodes and what it spares.

Letting Go:
thirty mourning sonnets and two poems

(2017)

Things We Leave Behind
after Cavafy

We knew it at once: the faded grooves
touched by the afternoon sun.
The crack where we'd left it too long
in the window, splitting the wood in two.
The candle wax we'd scrubbed but not removed.

Ah, yes, this table, it *was* our family.

We'd seen it last in the van from the charity,
shrouded by its empty, upturned chairs.
Now here it was in the newly-opened café
(had it been an office? No, the bakers…);
a resting-place for dust-blanched builders
slumped over strong tea, the full English,
as dark and heady as funeral incense.

They will always be around somewhere,
those worn-out things we leave behind…

On the other side, the place where she laughed
every birthday, all those festive lunches.
In the centre, the faint circle of a wine glass
abandoned to carry in warmed plates or dishes,
indelible now, an ever-bleeding blemish.

That afternoon, at 4 o'clock, we said goodbye
for one week only… I thought I'd see her.
And then that week became forever.

Lost
after Virgil

Up to that point, I was still in the dark.
I was retracing steps, staring down paths
I saw as ours, not thinking she had been
ripped from us already, had slipped unseen
as she sat down to rest. We'd just spoken –
I heard her laughing, hanging up the phone –
but when next we gathered, friends, family,
one of us would be missing, tricked away.
I bargained with gods I did not worship;
I blamed, I begged ambulance men, medics.
Reaching home, I tried to put on armour,
convincing myself that they had saved her,
that they had been in time, they had, they had...
In response there was only silence, dread.

Suppliants
ghosting Aeschylus

They had laid her out like a warrior,
placed a hand towel under slippered feet,
a doormat for head, shielded by her hair.
I knelt beside her, too soon yet to weep,
and, like a suppliant, I took her hand,
told her she was beautiful, loved, would be
always. This had been our sanctuary
but now we were fugitives, shored on land
we no longer knew. Now we spoke only
in laments, the savage language of hurt,
strangeness of mourning. Up ahead was dust,
the dirt cloud of an advancing army,
a whirl of axles churning up soft earth -
ruthless, muffled. And already on us.

Ring
for Dad

The last time he had held it in his hands
was Penzance, late nineteen-fifty-five. Storms
that roared around the church had for once ebbed;
coats were being unbuttoned, wool scarves shed.
Outside, my beaming mother had just stepped
from the car, poised between past life and next,
as the weight of a box in his best suit
became a bond, unbroken, resolute.

Tonight he twists it between taut fingers,
peering through its opened circle as if
a peephole into some new dimension
where all the days and years might not have been.
The door chimes: undertakers at the gate.
Now there's just one vow left for him to make.

Snow
after Homer

Out of nowhere, it flurries thick and fast,
early winter yet sharp as arrow shaft.
The wind calms. Grief is stilled. But it falls on
veiling the Forest hills, dark, distant Downs,
levelling fresh-ploughed farmland. By the church
it pales the priest's black coat as he clears paths
in vain, ghosts the bonnet of skidded hearse;
it dampens down crematorium furnace,
cuts off caterers, blocks would-be mourners.
Drifting further, across the south and west,
flakes catch on harbour walls like drying nets.
Now only the spray curved above Penzance
remains unblanched, grazed against those grey shores.
All else is wrapped in snow, stifled, silenced.

Glove

Among the scraps we find an outstanding
order, processed, which doesn't know to stop.
A week later, an oblong package drops
through the letterbox like some fresh offering
for the dead. Inside there's a pair of gloves,
black fleece, as if she had known we'd need them;
that this deep, early fall would be coming.
I scrunch my hand to find they fit, if snug,
and feel, once again, hers in mine, reaching
out to hold me safe, long past my childhood,
on main roads or slippery paths, guiding
me on as I laughed her off. Now I would
do anything to reach back, keep that hold
clasped round the unchanged centre of my world.

Ice
after Livy

All winter the earth tipped from under us;
we were balancing on sheer precipice,
with no way down or up. Beneath our feet
new snow had drifted on old, not too deep
yet soft, and the more we tried to progress,
the more it shrunk, the more it smoothed to slush
or compacted ice. Even if we crawled
on hands and knees, still we would falter, fall
without roots to cling on to, straws to hold,
each step an unyielding struggle. Below,
between the clouds, we saw our Forest streams,
the Downs lit by lowered sun; there, it seemed,
most lived their lives on solid, fertile ground.
For now we were trapped. Out of reach. Ice-bound.

Watch
Every day measures the same as the next…

A few months later my father spread out
some boxes on their bed – the jewellery
we'd helped him pick for anniversaries
and birthdays that we'd now no longer count.
I chose a pair of blue agate studs, sky
blanched, sea-washed, like her eyes. And her gold watch
so that I could still feel those same hours tick
on and on, the strict time that she'd lived by.
I wanted to think of her keeping score
of each lost second, holding that cold face
to the ear for one more, and then one more;
its hushed, imperceptible breath lasting
without end, nudging us back into place –
the soothing sound of her time still passing.

Thaw

after Livy

By now we were discouraged, exhausted.
We had set up camp on that same high ridge
yet were still on thin ice, with snow to dig
if we wanted to edge down, inch by inch.

And so we waited for the wind to change.
We stripped out dead undergrowth, gathered fuel,
used our bitterness to dissolve rock, flame
the glowing bracken and scorch a way through.

Turning back on ourselves, we eased the steep
gradients of the Forest, and then pushed
on round the valley slopes until we reached
the stream below in the shade of the woods.

Here we rested. At last this seemed somewhere
we could live. A softer landscape, gentler.

Fairfield Church

Our last trip. We were laughing as she picked
her way across the causeway in high heels
and smart suit. *Well, we're going for a meal...*
Below, the marsh channels coiled like the Styx
by which even our gods swear faith; the rust
that can break glass or stone, that will corrode
not just hard iron or lead but pearl and bones.

This time all the birds of Kent and Sussex
have fallen silent as if Avernus,
the poisoned gate to Hell, lay beneath us.
Blocking the way a few miles up the road
we find them all: a vast murder of crows,
their black wings locking like a drawbridge grill
as they rise up, screeching, to let us through.

By-pass
after Plato

I knew the place already. Even if
for a second, I had been there myself
as my own heart was stopped and then started
again, healed. Perhaps that was why we failed,
could only grasp at the shadows of those
we had come to save, taking the coward's
quest – or the poet's – seeking out pathos,
regret's raw matter, not willing to die
in our turn: tricksters who'd somehow contrived
a way to quit the gates of Hell alive.

So the gods sent punishment we deserved;
this quagmire grief that serves as its own curse.
The pain you cannot write through or by-pass.
That feels like too little love. Or too much.

Roman Road

Camp Hill. Clouds taut as guy-ropes tether land
to sky, steadying the heart. *The way up,*
as Heraclitus taught, *is the way down...*
Horses gallop past, churning up the scrub
on the road to Rome. *The dead are our friends,*
our colleagues, our fellow conspirators.
They, too, shape our waking world... Loss and gain.
Conquest and defeat. The spurred messengers
bringing word from each broken side. The same
time yet in a different time. Here it seems
those endless lines might cross and cross again.

A crow startles. Sheep rest on the heaped edge
as if warmed by hidden bones. *Still we dream*
our own locked dreams, the living and the dead.

Cleft

By a cliff top path where the grass is pressed
like the imprint of lovers' morning hair
or faded graveyard cross, there is a cleft –
Mary's word – that in Virgil or Homer
would lead to the Underworld, Erebus:
grief, disease, the horrors of its darkness,
but here is stopped by a sprig of late thrift,
a faded kiss to keep us from the brink.

At Botallack the mist slides out from field
and sea, infinity slowly revealed,
our own world returned, piece by fragile piece –
a place to stop the hurt, to lease back speech;
this necromancer's task of easing breath
into moss-flecked lungs of our long, long dead.

Seat

Even from the bench, the bay is undimmed;
beyond hazy blackthorn the Mount quivers
as its pine trees tilt, reeled back by the wind –
the marker that tells us we're really here
at the far point, lying low, facing west.
Below, rocks snag across a land on loan
from the turning tide, shrunk into darkness.
Nothing soothes the soul like the sight of home:
this one rears daughters fierce as fighting men.
Here's where you rested with your own mother
watching swifts dip, dissect the setting sun,
by paths picked out in selfheal and clover.
Blood and bone pack the sacred ground beneath:
your place. My longed-for Ithaca. Our seat.

Let Go
after Virgil

Those nights I called her name in vain again
and again, filled ruined cities with tears.
I dreamt I reached familiar streets, my fear
fixing tongue to roof of mouth, hair on end;
again she came to me through parted crowds,
smarter than ever in weathershield mac,
blood red lipstick and jaunty, matching hat
like a warrior plume. 'I can't stay long now,'
she said, 'yet am always here. Remember
to hold your hopes close, guard your ambition.
Love. Travel. Most of all, let go anger
or this exile of grief will be too long.'
I tried and tried and tried to embrace her
but, like a thought on waking, she was gone.

Star

So we come full circle to falling dusk.
Above Priest's Cove, the sky is darkening
through Brisons rocks, evening hesitating
between clouds and sea, cautious, on the cusp.
A shard of moon slips through, blurred with regret,
fresh votive to this place, our penitence
for the lost: parents, old friends and the house
we mourned as if a lover rashly left.

But the day has gone, its turning point passed.
Now the most beautiful of all the stars –
the evening star, shepherd star, Hesperus –
gathers all that light-tinged dawn has scattered;
it guides the fishing boats, herds in sailors,
sends daughters running home to their mothers.

Ghost Passage

(2022)

Writer [?], London
Writing tablets, Walbrook, London

It seems a slip, a novice error,
marked as if crossed through.
A name no one can read. Or knew.

But I am the first. It holds my fear
and my life, the heart-knot terror
of a letter misplaced, misconstrued.
I breathe through its blocked lungs –
my blood, my bone, my sinew.

And all those others yet to come.
Centuries later fold back each leaf
to trace the fossil frail we'll make,
this usury of borrowed tongues;
mud-stopped loans, gains of dust,
the lines we send like ash-bud moths
to brush your doorstep as you sleep:
We bear witness in our own hand
that debts owed shall be paid later…

We have seen our city shrink to sand
so we scratch wood to soothe the ache –
diminished words we leave behind
to score these shuddering, ghosted streets
back into form and place: *London writer.*

Then hand them on for you to shape.

The First European
Legionary tomb, Colchester, 49 CE

They never managed to pronounce my name;
as I'm tall, I was always 'Longinus',
'Lofty' (I'm Sdapeze, son of Matygus,
a Thracian from Sofia). Can't complain:
I was on double time. The days were dank
but the oysters were good. I bought a cloak
plus a fine hunting bitch, Agassia,
with squat little legs, sharp teeth and soft paws.
The wife and kids back home would have loved her.

Fifteen years I served with the cavalry
across the east – Syria, Scythia.
At forty it ends here. Remember me:
I was in the advance, one of the first.
Your ancestor. My bones still feed this earth.

Destruction Horizon
Walbrook, London, 60 CE

…to save a province, Suetonius sacrificed a city.…

On the streets, priests spoke of omens,
babbling voices in the lock-down basilica,
laughter rattling out from empty theatres,
a twin city reflected in the rising Thames.

I didn't waver. We didn't have the numbers.
I gave the command to march on. Some came.
Most were trapped by age or sex, a strange
allegiance to this border post, a tenderness
for hovels they somehow held as home.
They saw the dust storm spinning nearer,
carrying their own deaths – and the British.
A tally of thousands for that bitch Boudica.

But we left them a marker in memorial,
our destruction horizon: impacted soil,
a trickle of crimson soot like dried blood.
Dig down. Dig deep. It's soaked in the mud.

New Roman

Writing tablet, Walbrook, London, 61 CE

ABCDEFGHIKL
MNOPQRST…

In a charred shack we learn our lessons.

Through the smoke I can smell sorrel, ramsons,
blackthorn blossom drifting across like ash
as the shouts of soldiers shatter our hush
and wagons of the dead still roll on past.

We do not want this world, the old language:
destruction, put to fire, revolt, flight, death.
Our task is to etch a new alphabet –
new letters, new tools to rebuild our homes,
gardens for us children, games to play, schools.
We'll smooth the jagged edge of dialect
and salve its gaping wounds in majuscule.

A-B-C: the scorched march of New Roman
turning blackened wood into cold white stone.

Will

Writing tablet, Walbrook, London, 68 CE

I [insert name here] of the Vangion
First Cohort bequeath to my son:

The cries of butchers in the market halls,
haze of blacksmiths, hum of metalworkers;
a scent of spice from across the empire,
stench of piss trickling out from tanners' stalls.

The swell of every language: Gallic, Greek,
German, Numidian, Thracian, Phrygian.
The swagger of swollen businessmen
claiming their ownership of our coined streets.

The shade of gardens and hidden courtyards.
A breath-held stillness in the morning bars
as lonely veterans drain one last beer
by the bones of their half-built arena.

This brutal, brimful, unpredictable
city. The air we built it from. The will.

Thief
Writing tablet, Walbrook, London, 69 CE

for Attius the thief, at Rochester…

I knew it the first day I saw him.

A chill November morning, the sun
sharpening the room we'd stumbled
back to the night before; his small bed
at one end, a shelf for cracked Samian,
worn chair piled with clothes. The way
he peeled the stiff tunic from my body
murmuring my name as if it was his
to take. A sacred enchantment. A curse.
As if he'd always believed I'd come.
A client. In his debt. *Marcus. Marcus.*

Yes, I knew it. All was over. Lost.

Outside, the world spun. Emperors
changed by the hour. Our governors
fled. Now time was a breath suspended
between the dawn cries of forum traders
and rhythmic chants of recalled soldiers
falling away as the day scuttled to its end.
On the roof the tiles hissed with rain
while we made love over and over again.

Then one morning he said he was leaving.
Out in the market it was trying to snow.
Our sanctuary, too, had ice in the air:
he talked of Rochester, a new legion.
Rochester. The name was like poison.
I lay in bed all day trying to read, alone:
Ovid, Catullus, the passion of *Myrmidons*:
my love remember the nights we shared…
I saw his eyes, flecked with fiery topaz,
inhaled the scent of his hop-soaked skin.

Through the walls, someone coughed
or shuffled across the creaky floor above.
I read on. The city was empty. A husk.

Attius, you thief, come back to London.
Return it to me, the heart you have stolen.

Keepsake
Inscribed writing stylus, Walbrook, London, 75 CE

From Rome, a keepsake to bring you pleasure –
a pointed gift so you will always remember;
I wish I could have given you much, much more
but the journey is long and funds are short.

I'm sure he threw it in the stream. London,
I'd heard, was in ferment, packed with pleasure:
fine wines, sweet ale, and most of all women,
its frost-edged dusk a lure to warm the bones.

My message, sharpened, in miniature,
would go unread, unmarked. He didn't know
there was a further present still to come
from that brief, jasmined night he'd forgotten –
those pared hours we shared before he embarked –

but I relived by day; how the moon grazed
the sea at Ostia like a polished blade
as each serrated kiss cut time in half.

A keepsake to bring you pleasure. Ten days
old. Her father in replica. As sharp.

The House Opposite
Writing tablet, Walbrook, London, 80 CE

Give this note to the cooper Junius,
just opposite the house of Catullus…

I unpack my treasures of Syrian glass,
plates sourced from the slopes of Vesuvius.
The walls I paint with frail shoots of grass
and a poppy – my own hidden message
for those who know the poet, my namesake:
a flower fallen at the meadow's edge…

I had pictured myself as a pioneer
composing dark, difficult northern poems
as fêted (one day) as my famed forebear.
Besides I'd been priced out of Rome.

Yet each word I write I later delete.

I watch the starlings rising up at dusk
above the teeming, cloud-fogged streets
like a simile slipping out of grasp.
I hear the drunken Rhenish equites
chant their alehouse verse, swilled in vomit –
our bleak reward for seven months' back pay.
My voice is clogged with London clay.

All I am here is the house opposite
the cooper, two doors down from the brewer.
The only lines that come, come in error
and for them: barrels, bills, more calls for beer.

In Athens
Tombstone, Tower Hill, London, 100 CE

He said they were the most exquisite words
in any language. I can see him on the quay
bowing as he introduced himself, undeterred,
as if he knew, despite his age, such beauty
and grace would have us instantly enthralled.

It's true: his eyes were still a deep cerulean,
his smile calmed like a ship reaching landfall,
his face was a monument, one of the ancients.
Still he carried with him a trace of the Aegean
if he now spoke Greek with a slight Latin accent.

Aulus Alfidius Olussa. Even etched on a tomb
his name was an involuntary sigh. Or a poem
almost-made, nearing completion. Yet between
'70 years' and 'here lies' there was some room,
enough – surely just enough – to squeeze it in.
The only epitaph he required: *Born in Athens.*

Seafarer

Marble slab, Tabard Street, South London, 161 CE

To the Divine Emperors and Mars Camulus
Tiberinius Celerianus of the Bellovaci, Moritix,
Seafarer, the first Londoner to… [*dedicates this*]

They say that you always know the start
if not the end. I must have made a thousand
crossings, turbulent in our skiffs. On the first,
I remember, I was so sick the captain laughed.
Mid-sea, we were suddenly suffocated by fog.
We slowed to stillness. Time itself had stopped.
I could hear cries from unseen crafts like ghosts
trapped in their waterlogged worlds, warning us
to keep, to stay away. Suddenly we saw land,
cliffs through a cleft in the clouds. My captain
patted me on the back. Baptism, he said, by mist.

Now I am a captain myself, rank of *Moritix*:
Cross-Channel Seafarer, the first Londoner to.
Still I fear those freighted, moon-dragged
waters. I pray for protection to my own god,
Mars Camulus – and to the emperors, in lieu.
The first Londoner to…. The first… The first.

I make these offerings so I won't be the last.

Dark Earth
London, 420 CE

And then we lived like ghosts in our cities.

Decay crept outwards from centre to edge
but we held firm, jeering at those who fled.
Markets crashed so we buried our money.
Sickness shadowed us on the streets. We stayed
at home. In time we knew nothing of towns
beyond our own. Squares, gardens, all spare land
we turned to crops. Fights were stopped, games not played.
In the arena baiting bears ran free.

We are sinking back into History,
dark earth, the detritus of worn empires.
All we are. All we've been. All that matters.

We sow words in wood, through clay, on stone walls.
We know if we stay silent, darkness falls.

Ghost Passage
Kent, 553 CE

(*after Procopius*)

Late at night, they hear banging at their doors,
a voice, indistinct, calling them to task.
They do not shrink. They wake, walk to the shore
confused by their compulsion, or who asks,
compelled to act just the same. They find boats
like their own if not quite. Somehow other.

As they lift out the oars they feel the load
like lead ballast, a haul of passengers.
They see soaked planks lying low in the depths
of the waters, lapped to the very edge
of the rowlocks – barely a finger's breadth
above the surge – but no more, no one else.

Within a long hour they return to Kent,
Thanatos, isle of the dead. That tare weight
lifts. They hear nothing, no steps disembark
yet the same voice urges them to take charge
of these lost souls: all the ghosts of France, Spain,
Italy – and Britain. As each descends
their achievements are called in requiem.
Their kindness. Their partners, their parents' names.
Those they had loved. All those who had loved them.

from Oxney Sonnets

Bull
Roman altar stone, Stone-in-Oxney church

Once I was led through the streets garlanded
with flowers and rare jewels. Kings paid homage.
Philosophers shook at my touch. They said
that when I died, priests and seers shaved their heads
while stern dictators wept. I was their god
and their pet: Apis, Lord of Life. And Loss.

I prefer it here. That homesick sailor,
shivering for the heat of Alexandria,
who carved your rough Kent sandstone, set me free.
Now I am always mid-leap. Mugs of tea
warm my flanks. Stacked sheaves of parish minutes
serve as diadems for my head. I finish
your devotions, sing hymns with my dust breath.

I run with you into each mildewed death.

White
Isle of Oxney, Kent, May, 991

....this place also was by the Danes piteously spoiled and burnt...

After London, Oxney seemed so easy.

We slid through its streams by a marauders'
moon, a milk moon, to guide us in the dusk.
Everywhere blazed white – daisies, cow parsley,
horse chestnut candles – as if we had slipped
back in time to face a fierce new winter.
Above us, a penitent patch lingered
on the slopes; hawthorn drifted round its cliffs
like a late, phantom fall across the Marsh.

We pressed on. To us their timber houses,
each precious church, were no more than kindling
for our ice fires. And we prefer blood-red;
the only white we might want to see is
flickering, pure. At the edge of a flame.

Jazz

Stone-in-Oxney churchyard

Giuseppina
Nov. 6th 1914–19th May 1915

Look for my bugle-bound, three-quarter grave,
a breath-stop life. The four beat name we share
picked out in lead Grotesk: **GIUSEPINNA.**
I still keep time here, November to May,
as spring blossom's blown, chestnut candles damped
back down. **FOR SUCH IS THE KINGDOM OF GOD...**

In my six months I knew only war – Ypres,
Gallipoli – as I slept in my crib
dreaming of a great age. But that spring night
in Chicago, Tom Brown's Dixieland Band
first syncopated drums for their new sound,
too late for me, I faded from the fight.

I miss those note-pierced hours I never had.
Dancing. Laughter. Ragtime for ragwort. Jazz.

A Few Feet
Old Romney churchyard

A shorn-off column marks the breaths not spent
of *Joseph Reginald Herbert Cooper*
who *fell ill while serving his country…* Spring
nineteen-nineteen, the war six months over.
Aged Nineteen. Still it managed to claim him.
Beside him a burrow bound with green wire fence
holds *Sergeant W. J. Stephen, Air Gunner.*
Nineteen forty-four. Once again *Nineteen.*

As in the mess, they stretch out, ankles crossed,
arms behind heads, exchanging fags, pictures
of sweethearts and blotted, thumb-marked letters.
Or plan that swift one in The Rose & Crown
while words hang like stopped dandelion clocks

and the next war waits, just a few feet on.

Visitors' Book
Snargate church

Turning its pages, crinkled as damp skin,
we find her handwriting like an old friend
strangely met, out of context: *10/10/10.*
A day she's marked to perfection, looping
the joint '*D*'s in her name and my title,
still new then, even here the proud mother.
I reach down to release her snagged pleasure
to skim her soft, cupped hand: *So beautiful..*

...mould, plaster, *L'Air du Temps*, inhaled again,
the Doom Boards read aloud, the wall-daubed ship
nearly-sailed. Less than six weeks left with her
before our dates, our lines, will be taken
by these others, thickened with different scripts:
pilgrims, walkers, ancestor worshippers.

Archaeology of Home

(new poems)

Writing Cure

Thoth, the scribe-god, invented many arts
but the most important of these was writing…
(Plato, *Phaedrus*, 274d)

The Egyptian king was not impressed.
'An author,' he said, 'is not best placed
to judge their own creation. That task
falls to others. You insist this knowledge
will make our memories clearer, coherent.
Writing is a scourge, a wounding punch;
it increases forgetfulness by negligence.
If we trust the alphabet, this latest art –
strange, alien characters outside ourselves –
we will not recall our own true experience.
Your wonder cure cannot give us back our past;
it teaches us how to learn by rote and not by heart.'

Odysseus and Laertes

As if a stranger, he stared right through me.

I'd found him in the garden, dug in, filthy,
his shins patched against scuff or scratch,
tattered gloves for thorn guard, his old straw hat.
'Who are you?' he asked. 'How did you get here?'
Confused, he needed proof, signs to be sure.
I showed him the scar of a dog bite wound.
I numbered the trees he had walked me through
as a pestering child: cypress, low enough
then to leapfrog, now taller than the house;
crab apple for shade; laurels; fig bushes.
The yew where I had made my camps. Hedges
he'd grown to keep the world out and us in.

He smiled like buds surprised by early spring.

Geometric
(vase fragment collection, University of Birmingham)

Smooth as a draughtsman's or architect's bureau,
each drawer contains the blueprint of a place;
a shattered world whose stacked, disparate pieces
cannot be matched or reassembled into things.
A mnemonic for each dismantled city – Tiryns,
Mycenae – reduced to horizontal topology:
stopped meanders, unjoined dots, lone spirals;
parallel lines that no longer reach towards infinity.
A flash of familiar pattern. A ghost flower. A single
wave-crest breaking on a distant, childhood shore;
the stork that soared above the marshes, unexpected,
fleeting, like a thought begun and, at once, faded.

What rolls out of the waiting dark is not destruction
but disconnection. Through care home and hospital
my father had clutched his own memento: *Euclidean
Geometry.* Ariadne's thread. His passage back: *if equals
are subtracted from equals the remainders are equal…*
Here, in clay, all rules are now broken; the terrible
knowledge of what we no longer know. The angled path
to our shrinking past. *The whole is greater than the part.*

Daffodil Vase
(craft revival, late 1970s)

As if a faded Roman fresco, only the stalks are left.
I remember the day I bought it, a new student numb
with homesickness. Autumn. Those entrenched dusks
in a lost London: the fog-locked gates to the Museum

and scent of charred chestnuts on the coals outside
which no one ever seemed to buy; *Standard* bearers
reporting campaigns, strikes. Repurposed demolition sites.
On a stall by the boarded Market, I unearthed it for her

from clay: a Sussex spring, my mother's wildflower beds.
Forty years on, I'm in her back cupboard sinking trenches,
exhuming long-buried, deep-store Christmas presents.
The archaeology of home. Its heart-hollowing tenderness.

Catalogues, Various
(outdated)

For months they would arrive at his door
like persistent detectives or debt-collectors:
discount books, clothes, copies of *Esquire*;
tours abroad (his passport had long expired).

We'd cream off those that caught the eye:
Saga River Cruises, Great Rail Journeys –
the last big trip you think will heal or change.
In my dream travels I'm back to the end

masked again as if I planned a heist on death.
My father is still sitting up, still able to talk.
He slings me a brochure for The Far, Far North
slippery as verglas. *See*, he says, *I've already left*.

Reading the Signals
(Sea of Azov, Scythia, 513 BCE)

When the Persians ordered them to submit
the Scythians sent the invaders strange gifts:
a bird
> *a mouse*
>> *a frog*
>>> *&*
>>>> *five arrows*

(Herodotus, *Histories*, 4.131.)

The Persians pondered. 'Danger,' Gobryas,
the King's go-to man, declared. 'I know
that these gifts signal death for all of us:
unless we climb into the clouds like birds
or like mice dig ourselves into deep holes,
or like frogs slither into dank, dark water,
we will die. We will never see our homes.'

But the King disagreed. Here were gestures
of submission, he said. Conceding power.
As he spoke, the bird soared, scuttling the sky.
The mouse shuddered through his parted feet,
a shadow on the edge of sight. The frog
slid into a stagnant pool with a sigh.

Unbroken, he held the arrows like a forlorn
suitor clutching bud-less stems, rose-thorns
after the storm, the leavings of vast wars;
amaranthine ambition, cold as conceit,
sharp as a sneer. And pointing fleshwards.

Burying the Bones
(Teutoburg Forest, Germany, 15 CE)

Marching at the furthest frontier of empire,
the legions came to the site of the massacre…
(Tacitus, *Annals*, 1. 60)

We saw the flash of white first, scattered
over fields or heaped like shovelled snow.
We walked on slaughter. Shards shattered –
skull scraps, spine slivers – beneath the groves

as the light congealed. Decomposed heads,
hacked from the corpses of fellow soldiers,
hung like roosting bats or a rotting harvest,
their mouths drooping in a howl of horror.

By now we could not tell which was joined
with which. But we collected up those parts
like family, like strangers, lovers mourned
too soon; blood of our blood, buried at last.

In grief and rage we wept as if for old friends
at the confusion of war, the cost. At how it ends.

Preparing to Meet the Dead
(Boscawen-ûn Stone Circle, West Penwith: June)

At the half-way point, yards out, it quivers
between granite and air, drawing you on.
Clouds guard its gateway like charging dragons;
inside, the stones quake with umbellifers,
loitering bluebells. A central shaft leans east
towards a grave slumped in its own passage;
a signpost for the lost – to Tartarus –
pointing out the way with its carved bare feet.

In a few weeks' time I would cross their paths
while a pump breathed for me. I'd feel their loss
of bone. How a heart unbeats. That rib-gap.
They would lead me home, teach me how to tread
in the cold, stone-seared footsteps of the dead
that take us forward by tearing us back.

Worth
(St Nicholas Church, West Sussex: November)

We come as converts, as if the first time
or as pilgrims, the last of many times.
We are South Saxons, Northmen. The conquered.
Conquerors. We have oak for bone, packed mud
for blood. Through hacksaw hum and bonfire haze,
rib-caged limes lead to the Confessor's nave;
horse hooves clatter on a prayer-smoothed chancel,
earls making obeisance before battle

a wounded king craving absolution.
Wyrd changes the changing world. Time folds. Then.
Now. Every year for the last thousand
the sun has brushed the glass to spot the stones
just here: viridian, cobalt, crimson…
Each has their worth. But light still wanes. Moves on.

Notes & Sources

from *CHASING CATULLUS:*
POEMS, TRANSLATIONS AND TRANSGRESSIONS
i.m. Rachel Evans (15/9/1988-2/8/1996)

'78 NIGHTS:
A version of C.P. Cavafy's 1907 poem 'One Night', which, like Cavafy himself, speaks Greek 'with a slight British accent'.

FEMININE ENDING: TO SULPICIA:
Scholars have often attributed the Latin poet Sulpicia's handful of surviving poems to her male contemporary Tibullus. Restored to its rightful owner in more recent years, her witty, erotic verse is the only known example of women's poetry from classical Rome.

the year one: Sulpicia was writing around the turn of the 1st century BCE/first century CE.

Sulpicia est: 'this is Sulpicia'.

your name ends in… feminine proper nouns in Latin usually end in '-a', while their masculine counterparts end in '-us'.

AFTER TITIAN'S *BACCHUS AND ARIADNE*:
Quotation from *Critische Dichtkunst* ('Critical Poetics') by Johann Christoph Gottsched (collected and translated in *Translation/History/Culture: A Sourcebook*, edited by André Lefevere (Routledge, 1992). Titian's 1522 painting 'Bacchus and Ariadne' depicts the moment when the god catches sight of Ariadne on Naxos. Deserted by her lover, Theseus, after helping him to escape from the Minotaur's maze, a distraught Ariadne turns away towards a crown of stars, while Bacchus, surrounded by his orgiastic revellers, leaps down from his chariot towards her, overwhelmed by wild passion. Frank Auerbach's 1971 painting 'After Titian's Bacchus and Ariadne' reworks Titian original in abstract expressionist style, turning Titian's delicately worked characters into rigorous girders of colour.

Beyond, the faithful…: this passage, based on Catullus, 64.254-64, was Titian's starting point for his painting.

sacred point: a stroke of the thyrsus, the sacred rod carried by Bacchic revellers, was said to induce ritual frenzy.

dust-bowl caskets: containing the cult's sacred serpents and other ritual paraphernalia.

PHILOMELA:
In Greek myth, Philomela was raped by her brother-in-law, Tereus, who cut out her tongue in order to stop her from revealing his crime. But Philomela depicted her ordeal in a tapestry which she then sent to her sister Procne. On discovering the truth about Tereus, Procne murdered their son Itys, serving his flesh up to his father at a feast. The gods later turned the sisters into birds, a swallow and a nightingale.

DE RAPTU PROSERPINAE:
Based on *Claudian* 3.231-44.
Claudian's unfinished epic poem of c.400 CE describes how Proserpina (the Latin form of Persephone), daughter of the corn-goddess Ceres or Demeter, was abducted by Pluto, god of the Underworld.

NIOBE:
Based on a Chorus from Sophocles' tragedy *Antigone* (823-31). Niobe, who had seven sons and seven daughters, boasted that she was therefore superior to Leto, mother of Apollo and Artemis. When the twin gods killed all her children in punishment, Niobe's grief turned her to stone.

CANCEL THE INVITE II:
Based on Plato, *Republic*, 398a. All but the most morally stern poets were to be banned from Plato's utopian city.

If you came…: the translation was inspired by lines 21-31 of T.S. Eliot's poem 'Little Gidding' from *Four Quartets* (Faber and Faber, 1944).

SET IT IN STONE:
The first two sections are based on ancient funerary inscriptions.

DEMETER IN WINTER:
After the abduction of her daughter (see note on '*De Raptu Proserpinae*' above), Demeter wandered the earth in search of her, until the king of

the gods, Zeus (Jupiter), granted that the child should be restored to her mother, provided she had not eaten any food in the Underworld. But as Persephone (Proserpina) had eaten six grains of a pomegranate, Zeus ruled that she should spend six months of the year with her mother and six months in the Underworld, during which time Demeter mourned her loss, bringing winter to the earth.

IN COVENTRY:
On the night of November 14, 1940, Coventry's ancient cathedral was destroyed by German bombers. A new cathedral, designed by Sir Basil Spence, was consecrated on May 25, 1962, and has subsequently become known for its ministry of forgiveness and reconciliation.

angels…etched: John Hutton's vast glass entrance screen, engraved with angels, divides the new cathedral from the ruins of the old.

Gethsemane: the Chapel of Christ in Gethsemane, to the right of the Lady Chapel.

Piper's Light: the stained-glass Baptistery windows, designed by John Piper.

Sutherland… shrine: Graham Sutherland designed the altar tapestry of Christ in Glory.

FRESH MEAT:
A version of *Iliad* 22 (25-360, condensed), commissioned by the journal *perversions*, and based on Homer's account of the single combat between the Greek hero Achilles and the Trojan champion Hector, as Achilles seeks to avenge his fellow-warrior and lover Patroclus, whom Hector has slain. The poem plays on the Greek's homoerotic sub-text, not just of Achilles' love for Patroclus but also the subconscious undercurrent of desire between the two opposing warriors, particularly in a speech by Hector, translated here (even if it is almost certainly a scribe's later interpolation). Drawn by Hector's ascribed words, I decided to pervert my version with this reading, changing the distanced, third-person narrative of Homer's epic into the first person lament of Hector's ghost.

death waits…slim ankle-joint: as a baby, Achilles had been bathed by his mother, Thetis, in the river Styx, making him immortal – except for the ankle she'd used to hold him. He was later slain at the Gates of Troy by an arrow shot into this ankle by the Trojan price Paris.

SCILLY:
Based on Odysseus' encounter with the Lotus-Eaters, in whose land he and his men arrive after sailing from Troy. As Odysseus later explains: 'whoever of them ate the honey-sweet fruit of the lotus had no longer any wish to return… these men I brought back to the ship under compulsion, weeping…' (*Odyssey*, 9. 94-97).

EASTER IN SANCREED:
Inspired by *Odyssey* 11 or the 'Book of the Dead' in which Odysseus descends into the Underworld. Sancreed is a village in west Cornwall where my ancestors are buried.

LETCHWORTH CREMATORIUM:
In *Odyssey* Book 11 (24-43) Odysseus follows the sorceress Circe's instructions and summons the ghosts of the dead at the entrance to the Underworld.

RETURN TO ITHACA (VIA CAVAFY):
mother: Odysseus' mother, Anticlea, had died of grief before he reached home – he meets her ghost in the Underworld.

father planting out his grief: during his absence, Odysseus' father, Laertes, kept to his country farm, nursing his grief alone.

wife whose heart unravels: besieged by suitors in his absence, Odysseus' wife, Penelope, devised a scheme to stall them; promising her admirers that she would choose one of them when she had finished her tapestry, she then unpicked it each night.

dog who's had its day: Odysseus' faithful dog, Argos, dies on his master's return.

lovers' bones: on his return Odysseus kills the suitors and their accomplices.

from *THE WORD FOR SORROW*

In his exile poetry, *Tristia* or 'Sorrows', the Roman poet Ovid (43 BCE-c.17 CE) details the hardships and deprivations of his exile from Rome to the wintry Black Sea city of Tomis, at the end of his known world. The collection explores Ovid's – or, to use the name he calls himself, Naso's – story, alongside that of an old, second-hand dictionary being used to translate his verse. Here, a faded name linked on its flyleaf in January 1900, and a chance Google search, led to a British captain in the doomed 1915/16 Gallipoli campaign of the First World War, near to Ovid's own place of exile on the Black Sea.

HAIL:
Perseus: the Tufts University digital classical library, dictionaries and resources website (www.perseus.tufts.edu).

G.A. Lyneham-Forsythe: for privacy, I have changed this name.

NASO ALL AT SEA:
Based on *Tristia* 1.2. (edited).

DANCING IN THE DARK:
Writing poems . . . : based on Ovid, *Epistulae ex Ponto*, 4.2.32-4.
Gallipoli…: the 1915 British campaign on the Gallipoli peninsula in western Turkey during the First World War was one of the conflict's most brutal, leading to 550,000 Allied and Turkish casualties, and ending in a humiliating defeat and retreat for Britain.

MALVERN ROAD STATION, CHELTENHAM I: APRIL 1915:
a merry bunch . . . : based on the caption for a photograph which appeared in *The Gloucester Journal*, April 17th 1915.

the men and I drink weak tea…: based on letters home from E.T. (Tim) Cripps in August 1915, then a lieutenant with the Royal Gloucester Hussars at Suvla Bay. The letters are held in the Gloucestershire Archives (D4920/2/2/3/4). See www.gloucestershire.gov.uk/archives.

MALVERN ROAD STATION, CHELTENHAM II: FEBRUARY 2005:
Catullus' flower….: an image from Catullus 11, where the flower is left at a meadow's edge to be 'touched and then devoured/by the passing plough'.

LANDED:
Based on the eye-witness accounts of Charles Bean in 'The Story of Anzac', *Official History of Australia in the War of 1914–18, Vols I & II* (Angus &

Robinson, 1938: 679) and Ellis Ashmead-Bartlett, *The Uncensored Dardanelles* (Hutchinson, 1928: 189–90), war diaries quoted in L.A. Carlyon, *Gallipoli* (Doubleday, 2002: 556; 585) as well as Harvey Broadbent, *Gallipoli: The Fatal Shore* (Viking, 2005: 234).

BETWEEN THE LINES:
Based on a letter by E.T. Cripps (see previous note on 'Malvern Road Station, Cheltenham I').

NASO WRITES HIS OWN EPITAPH:
Based on *Tristia* 3.3. (edited).

AMONG THE GRAVES: GREEN HILL, GALLIPOLI:
The isolated Commonwealth War Graves Commission cemetery at Green Hill on Gallipoli is where the (mostly unidentified) British dead from the Suvla battles are buried.

LAST ORDERS:
It should be our feast day at home . . . : based on a letter by E.T. Cripps (see note above on 'Malvern Road Station, Cheltenham I').

faded handbill: a poster from October 1914, announcing the Gloucestershire pubs where recruitments would take place.

DICTIONARY DEFINITIONS:
Construct the landscape . . . : based on *Tristia* 4.2.37–43 (edited).

NASO SEES ACTION:
Based on *Tristia* 4.1 (edited).

WELCOME NOTE:
Based on a letter by E.T. Cripps, reminiscences of Tony Fagan in Maurice Shadbolt (ed.), *Voices of Gallipoli* (Hodder & Stoughton, 1988: 21) and photographs in Broadbent (2005: 239 & 243).

black hair bleached/to white…: See *Tristia* 4.8.1–2.

SEEKING QUARTER I: NASO:
Based on *Tristia* 4.4. 49–54; 61–4.

SEEKING QUARTER II: GEOFFREY
We can't advance…: quoted by Carlyon (2002: 627).

AMONG THE GRAVES: SALONICA:
The largely forgotten Salonica campaign was fought against the Turks in Greece, Serbia, Albania and Bulgaria from 1915–18; for every death in battle, it's said, three more men died of malaria or dysentery.

War Graves certificate: the Commonwealth War Graves Commission website offers printable commemorative 'certificates' for all the 1.7 million Commonwealth soldiers buried abroad since 1914, which includes a photograph of the cemetery (https://www.cwgc.org/).

Edward Balmer: my great-uncle, who served with The King's (Liverpool), is buried at the Sarigol Military Cemetery, Kriston, 25 miles north of Thessaloniki.

NASO THE BARBARIAN:
Based on *Tristia* 5.7.

who is the barbarian here…: see *Tristia* 5.10. 37-44.

THE PENNY POT:
he served twice…: miners, like my great-grandfather, were in great demand in the army both during and after the First World War, firstly to dig out and shore up trenches and tunnels and later to recover the dead from them.

from *THE PATHS OF SURVIVAL*

Aeschylus' lost tragedy *Myrmidons* notoriously depicted the doomed love of the Greek hero Achilles for his fellow warrior Patroclus. All that now survives of the work are ten tiny fragments, found mostly in scraps of papyrus excavated in Oxyrhynchus in Egypt, or from quotations in other, later ancient writers. The collection follows their story, and of those who were touched by them, backwards through time, from the present-day to Aeschylus revising the play on his deathbed in 456 BCE.

PROEM: FINAL SENTENCE:
Oxyrhynchus Papyrus 2256 contains nearly 90 scraps of papyrus; of these, number 55 is a barely legible, five-line piece, although its words could read

'*kata skoton*' or 'into darkness'. It is thought these words might be part of the lover's lament Achilles murmurs over Patroclus' dead body in *Myrmidons*, later quoted by Lucian (See '*Erotic Tales*'). The fragment also appears in 'Blot'.

THE LIBRARIANS' POWER:
Inspired by an article by Zainab Bahrani with photographs by Roger LeMoyne in *Document* (Spring/Summer 2013).

THE STUDENT'S FIND:
A fragmentary piece of papyrus excavated in Oxyrhynchus by an Italian team in the 1930s appears to reveal the moment in *Myrmidons* that Achilles finally speaks out after his long silence onstage, sulking at his treatment by Agamemnon.

our stout spiv…: surviving photographs of the dig director, Evaristo Breccia, show him very smartly-dressed on site.

REDACTION:
John Anthony Cramer (1793–1848) was an Oxford classical scholar and later Dean of Carlisle Cathedral. His *Anecdota Parisina* collected together rare classical quotations from works in the collection of the Royal Library in Paris, including a line from *Myrmidons* (also found in Photius' *Lexicon*) although Cramer does not list the line's textual origin or its author. The poem also refers to the unrest in Paris during the radical uprisings of 1834 and their harsh suppression.

THE CLERK'S CRUSADE:
The siege of Constantinople during the Fourth Crusade in 1203–4 saw Christian pitted against Christian, as mutinous forces from the western or Latin church attacked the eastern city of Constantinople, drawn by its famous riches. Vivid eye-witness accounts – such as that by Niketas Akominatos – describe how, on 12th April 1204, the Latins breached the city walls by burrowing holes just big enough for single soldiers to crawl through. For three days they looted the city, destroying its Library and melting down its golden treasures to cart away. After the siege, Byzantine Greek successor states were set up in Nicaea and northern Greece where rescued works were taken for safekeeping.

GERARD'S CONSTELLATIONS:
Gerard of Cremona (1114–1187) was the leading scholar at the medieval Toledo School of Translators, translating Arabic versions of Greek scientific works into Latin, making them available again to the west after they had been preserved for centuries by the Arab world. In 1175 he translated Ptolemy's *Almagest*, a Greek mathematical and astronomical treatise, and one of the most influential scientific works of all time. Such translations were the forerunners of the rediscovery of Greek and Latin literary works during the Renaissance.

AMR'S LAST WORDS:
Amr ibn al-As (585–664), the Arab conqueror of Egypt, was also renowned as a poet and scholar. Some sources record that, on the orders of his Caliph, he destroyed any remaining secular works in the Library of Alexandria although most of its contents had probably already been lost, bit by bit, in various incidents over the centuries including Julius Caesar's accidental burning of the Library in 48 BCE and the Christian riots of 391 CE (see 'The Christians' Cheek'). A translation of Amr's dying words can be found in E.M. Forster's *Alexandria: A History and A Guide* (1922).

THE CHRISTIANS' CHEEK:
After their brief promotion during the reign of Julian (331–363), pagan rites were finally outlawed in 391 by the Christian emperor Theodosius. In Alexandria, bishop Theophilus and an angry mob of fellow Christians took the opportunity to attack a group of pagans who had taken refuge in the city's Serapeum – a Greek temple which had become an offshoot of the Great Library of Alexander and a centre of philosophical learning. After many street skirmishes, the Christians emerged victorious and it is thought they then destroyed many of the precious works in the Serapeum.

EROTIC TALES:
Lucian of Samosata (c.125–c.200) wrote the first novels in western history, including a prototype sci-fi adventure which sees its protagonists travel to the Moon. The authorship of his dialogue *Erotes*, or 'Erotic Tales', has been questioned but the work debates the difference in heterosexual and homosexual love, concluding the latter is superior. To further the argument, various literary works are quoted including a line from *Myrmidons*, although Lucian does not mention the author and play, presumably because both were so well known at the time.

MARGIN:
Didymus (c.63 BCE–CE 10) was an ancient Greek scholar and textual commentator who earned his nickname 'Chalcenterus' or 'Iron-guts' for the number of works he could digest. The Athenian comic playwright Aristophanes (446–386 BCE) often parodied Greek tragedies in his satires.

THE FERRYMAN'S ROLL:
According to many sources, including Galen (Hippocrates, 3.2), Ptolemy III (280–222 BCE) was so eager to collect books for the Library at Alexandria that he ordered any found on ships in the city's harbour to be seized (and listed 'from the ships') so that new copies would be made from the manuscripts which would then be returned intact. But when Athens sent him their great tragic works, including those of Aeschylus, Ptolemy kept the originals and sent back the copies instead. The lines from *Myrmidons* quoted here are among its most impenetrable, probably referring to the burning of the Greek ships by the Trojans after Achilles' refusal to fight, and are known to us from bemused parodies in Aristophanes' plays *Frogs* and *Peace*. The poem's ferryman Charon is a fictional character but the Hellenistic poet Callimachus (310–240 BCE) was employed at the Library and wrote a bibliographical survey of its works.

AESCHYLUS' DESK:
According to Lucian, Dionysius the Elder, tyrant of Syracuse (432–367 BCE), aspired to be a tragic poet and supposedly acquired Aeschylus' 'writing desk' for inspiration. His efforts were apparently atrocious although any who criticised his work were severely punished. The tricksters (and also would-be poets), Sarpedon and Diomedes, are fictional characters.

AESCHYLUS' REVISION:
Aeschylus' early work, *Persians*, draws on his experiences as a young man in defending Athens against the Persian invasion at the battle of Marathon in 490 BCE. The tyrant Hiero of Syracuse later invited Aeschylus to revive *Persians* in Sicily where, on a subsequent visit, Aeschylus is said to have died in 456 BCE. Cynaegirus is sometimes portrayed in ancient sources as Aeschylus' brother. Herodotus (6.114) tells how he was a hero of Marathon who attempted to hold back the stern of a Persian ship with his bare hands until they were cut off by an enemy axe.

from *LETTING GO:*
THIRTY MOURNING SONNETS AND TWO POEMS
i.m. Darlene Balmer (1934–2010)

THINGS WE LEAVE BEHIND:
After *The Afternoon Sun* (1919) by C.P. Cavafy.

LOST:
After Virgil, *Aeneid*, 2.735-57. As Troy falls to the Greeks, the fleeing Trojan prince Aeneas realises that his wife, Creusa, is missing.

SUPPLIANTS:
Lines 4-14 trace Aeschylus, *Suppliant Women*,180-202. In the play, the 50 daughters of Danaus, known as the Danaides, flee forced marriages in Egypt to seek sanctuary in the Greek city of Argos; on landing, Danaus sees a welcoming party advancing towards them, unsure if it is hostile or friendly.

SNOW:
After Homer, *Iliad*, 12.278-86. Homer's epic simile compares the missiles of the Greeks raining down on a besieged Troy to snow falling across the land.

ICE:
After Livy, *History of Rome*, 21.36-7. During Hannibal's march on Rome in 218 BCE, the Carthaginian troops become trapped on an impassable precipice in the snowbound Alps.

WATCH:
Title quote from Heraclitus fragment 106.

THAW:
After Livy, *History of Rome*, 21, 37. As Hannibal's troops at last find a way down from the Alps by clearing paths in the snow and melting rockfalls with brushwood fires, they add vinegar from their rations to degrade the stones before hacking a way through to lower ground.

FAIRFIELD CHURCH:
Lines 5-7 after Pausanias, *Description of Greece*, 8.18.5.
Fairfield Church is an isolated chapel on Romney Marsh, near Rye, East Sussex.

Avernus: a lake in southern Italy, whose name means 'bird-less', and was believed to have been the entrance to the Roman Underworld.

BY-PASS:
After Plato, *Symposium*, 179d. Plato accuses Orpheus of cowardice since, rather than dying in his wife's place, he attempted to return alive from the Underworld with Eurydice.

ROMAN ROAD:
Embedded quotes from Heraclitus fragments 60, 75 & 89.

Camp Hill: a clump of trees on the Ashdown Forest, East Sussex, where a part of the London-Lewes Roman road is visible.

CLEFT:
Inspired by a photograph by Alistair Common.
Botallack: a coastal mining village in west Cornwall.

SEAT:
Lines 1-8 are after Homer, *Odyssey*, 9.21-8. At the court of the Phaeacian king, Alcinous, Odysseus speaks of his longing for his homeland Ithaca.

The seat is on the costal footpath between Marazion and Perranuthnoe in west Cornwall.

LET GO:
After Virgil, *Aeneid*, 2.768-94. As Aeneas desperately searches Troy for his missing wife, Creusa's ghost appears to him, telling him to move on to Rome without her.

STAR:
Lines 9-14 from Sappho fragments 104b & 104a (based on my translations in *Sappho: Poems & Fragments*, revised ed., Bloodaxe Books, 2018, p.113).

Priest's Cove: a small beach below Cape Cornwall near St Just-in-Penwith in west Cornwall.

from *GHOST PASSAGE*

Poems based on the Bloomberg writing tablets were inspired by the cache of tablets found during excavations at the Bloomberg London Building, 2010–14. I am indebted to Roger Tomlin for his decipherment and edited commentary, *Roman London's first voices: Writing Tablets from the Bloomberg excavation, 2010–14* (MOLA, 2016). All Bloomberg tablets are annotated WT followed by their edition number.

RIB = *The Roman Inscriptions of Britain Vols I–III* (Alan Sutton/Oxbow, 1965–2009).

Apart from a few dated writing tablets and known historical events, dates given for the poems are estimations, based on archaeological reports.

WRITER[?], LONDON:
(for Charlotte 'Lottie' Parkyn)
Bloomberg WT 18 contains the Latin word '*Londinio*' and possibly also '*scriba*', a secretary or writer, the first recorded mention of the profession in London, although the word appears to have been scratched through as if written in error. The poem also quotes WT 55, a loan note.

frail: a leaf skeleton where only the vein network remains (see Robert Macfarlane, *Landmarks*, Hamish Hamilton, 2015: 309).

THE FIRST EUROPEAN:
The tombstone of the Thracian cavalryman, Longinus Sdapeze, was found in Colchester in 1928 (RIB. 201). Its early date, just a few years after Claudius's invasion in 43 CE, suggests Longinus was one of the emperor's own troops. It tells us that he was of the rank of *duplicarius* which meant he received twice the basic rate of pay. The tombstone is now on display in the Colchester Castle Museum.

Agassia: As well as oysters and wool, Britain was famous for its Agassian breed of hunting dogs.

DESTRUCTION HORIZON:
Head quote from Tacitus, *Annals*, 14.33.
In archaeology a destruction horizon is a layer of earth containing ash, soot and burnt artefacts denoting a past catastrophic event. During Boudica's

revolt in 61 CE, Suetonius Paulinus, the governor of Britain, decided to abandon London, although he later defeated the rebellious British tribes to the north of the city. The horizon left by Boudica's subsequent sack of London is still apparent in the city's archaeology. The poem draws on the accounts of Tacitus and Dio Cassius (*Histories*, 62.1), particularly the omens that presaged Boudica's destruction of the city.

NEW ROMAN:
Bloomberg WT 79 is scored simply with letters of the Roman alphabet, possibly used for teaching literacy. Its early date suggests that London recovered swiftly from Boudica's revolt.

WILL:
Bloomberg WT 48 appears to be the beginning of a legal Will. The Vangiones were a cohort raised from the German tribe of the same name.

THIEF:
Bloomberg WT 59 could be a fragment of a legal document or even a curse. But, as Roger Tomlin suggests, it could also be seen as a tease between friends (or, as here, lovers). The tablet can be broadly dated between c.62–70 CE but pinned down in the poem to 69 CE, a disruptive year of civil war in which four emperors were appointed in rapid succession. In Britain, the governor Trebellius Maximus unceremoniously left the province after a legionary mutiny.

Myrmidons: Aeschylus' fifth-century BCE tragic masterpiece (see notes on *The Paths of Survival* above). The line quoted is based on fragment 135.

KEEPSAKE:
(for Elena Theodorakopoulos)
A stylus, engraved on its four sides, discovered at Walbrook during the Bloomberg excavations. As Roger Tomlin notes, its message is along the lines of: 'I went to Rome and all I got you was this pen.'

THE HOUSE OPPOSITE:
Bloomberg WT 14 contains only an address on the outer face of the tablet. It has been sent to Junius the Cooper, or barrel-maker, whose premises are identified by his neighbour Catullus, making the latter the earliest named householder in London. His name recalls the great Roman poet, Gaius Valerius Catullus, who was a contemporary of Julius Caesar and made

rather derogatory mention of Britain in his verse, leading to the imagined connection with this later, British Catullus. The poem quotes a line from Catullus poem 11.

IN ATHENS:
(for Paschalis Nikolaou)
RIB. 9 was found in Tower Hill in 1852. The Latin wording *na[tus]Atheni[s]* or 'Born in Athens' was added in much smaller lettering, squashed between the final two lines, at the same time as the rest of the inscription. The stone is now in the British Museum.

SEAFARER:
RIB. 3014, an inscribed slab found in Tabard Street, presents a fascinating mix of Roman and Celtic culture. It contains the first known use of the term 'Londoner' as a noun (Latin: *Londiniensium*). The rare Latin word *moritix* is apparently derived from a Celtic word for 'seafarer', and applied specifically to Gauls trading across the Channel between Britain and Europe. Tiberinius the seafarer's tribe, the Bellovaci, are from a Belgic area west of Reims, while Mars Camulus is a typical blending of a Roman god with a local Celtic deity. The slab is now on display in the Museum of London.

DARK EARTH:
An archaeological horizon or layer of soil covering many sites of late Roman London. It is unclear whether its presence indicates abandonment or continuous occupation.

bears ran free: A fragment of a brown bear skeleton has been unearthed from the site of the London arena or amphitheatre at Guildhall, raising the suggestion that the rewilded arena might have been used for bear hunting.

GHOST PASSAGE *(for Liam Guilar)*
Based on Procopius, *On the Wars*, 8.20. 47–58.
Procopius recounts that he learnt this story from British travellers included in a Frankish embassy to the court of Justinian in Byzantium. It is possible that, hearing of an 'Isle of the Dead', Procopius might have confused the Greek for death (*thanatos*) with the Isle of Thanet which he might have seen on Roman maps.
    A tiny carved cameo seal, dating from the third century CE and found on the Thames foreshore, depicts a ghostly Roman rowing boat with four

sailors. It is now on display in the Museum of London.

from OXNEY SONNETS: (*for Paul Dunn*)
BULL:
The altar, now housed in the church tower of St Mary the Virgin Church, Stone-in-Oxney, Kent, is carved with a bull and oxen. It was previously thought to be from a temple of Mithras but is now believed to depict the Egyptian bull god Apis, worshipped by soldiers across the Roman empire. It was excavated from the church nave in the early 18th century and probably came from the nearby Roman fort of Lympne.

WHITE:
Head quote from Sir William Lombard, *A Perambulation of Kent* (1570).

milk moon: The full moon of May.
penitent: 'a spike or pinnacle of compact snow… left standing after differential melting of a snowfield' (*Landmarks,* Robert Macfarlane, Hamish Hamilton, 2015: 89).

JAZZ:
that spring night: on 15 May 1915, the first use of the term 'Jazz' may have come from Tom Brown's Band from Dixieland as they began performing in Chicago and started advertising themselves as a 'Jass Band'.

VISITORS' BOOK:
(*i.m. Darlene Balmer*)
Seven 18th century oval text boards, with dire Biblical warnings, are displayed on the nave arches of St Dunstan's Church, Snargate on Romney Marsh. It also has a fragmentary wall painting of a 'great ship' from c.1500 on the north wall.

from *ARCHAEOLOGY OF HOME (NEW POEMS):*

WRITING CURE:
According to Plato (*Phaedrus*, 274e-275b), Socrates relates how the invention of writing by the Egyptian god Thoth did not impress the king, Thamus, who was tasked with spreading the knowledge throughout Egypt.

ODYSSEUS AND LAERTES:
After his homecoming to Ithaca, Odysseus is reunited with his confused father, Laertes (*Odyssey*, 24. 226-31; 297-301; 320-45).

GEOMETRIC:
The vase fragments, in the archaic or 'geometric' style, date from 900–700 BCE, and were donated to the University of Birmingham's Archaeology Collection by the archaeologist Lady Helen Waterhouse in 1974.

READING THE SIGNALS:
Herodotus (*Histories*, 4.131-132) recounts how, as the Persians tried to conquer ancient Scythia (now part of modern Ukraine), they demanded signs of obeisance. Instead, the Scythians sent strange gifts which the Persians struggled to interpret.

BURYING THE BONES:
Tacitus (*Annals*, 1. 61-62) recounts how, six years after Germanic tribes had ambushed and slaughtered three Roman legions in the Teutoburg Forest in September 9 CE, the Roman general Germanicus visited the site of the battle.

PREPARING TO MEET THE DEAD:
Boscawen-Un stone circle, near St Buryan in west Cornwall, dates from the Bronze Age, and has nineteen upright stones with a central pillar which leans north-east towards a few flat slabs, possibly a collapsed Neolithic passage tomb on the edge of the site. Recently Neolithic carvings have been discovered on this pillar, including a large pair of bare feet, soles outwards, toes set upwards.

WORTH:
St Nicholas Church in Worth, West Sussex, one of the oldest Anglo-Saxon churches in England, dates to 950 CE, and is said to have been founded by Edward the Confessor. Its high-arched doors are believed to have allowed knights to ride in and out of church on horseback to pray at the altar before battle without dismounting. Legend also has it that King Harold retreated to the church after the Battle of Hastings in 1066.

Wyrd changes…: quote from 'The Wanderer', ll.107-8 (in Anglo-Saxon, 'wyrd' means the inevitable movement of time; Fate).

.